HOW TO
LOVE A MAN
FOREVER

Man Forever, can help turn an incompetent spouse to a helpful and successful marriage partner and home builder.

—Deacon John Dara
Christian Social Activist and
Management Consultant
Abuja, Nigeria

This isn't just another book on marriage...having read through, we can boldly say the content is divinely inspired all the way and that it is one of the very few practical books on the concept and institution of marriage.

—Opeyemi and Adenike Onifade
Abuja, Nigeria

I commend *How to Love a Man Forever* to every woman young or old. The book is an exposé on little things we should do, but we tend to overlook, which can spice up our marriage the godly way.

—Dr. (Mrs.) Ngeri S. Benebo
Director General/Chief Executive
NESREA, Nigeria

It is only to be expected that all God-loving and God-fearing Christians should be profoundly concerned at the sorry state of an ever-growing number of marriages in the Church. Leading a crusade for the healing of fractured and strained marital relationships as well as for the enthronement of time-tested values for marital and family enrichment—"one marriage at a time"—is Olapeju Otsemobor's *How to Love a Man Forever*.

Within a mere thirty minutes of this book getting into my hands (coming, as it were, as a personal gift to me from the author's pastor), I felt compelled to call up the author (whom I had never met) to express my deep appreciation for her efforts in bringing forth such a practically incisive work on one of the most challenging aspects of human and/or Christian life.

I heartily recommend this book to the Church and to the world. In doing so, I pray that it would be greatly used of God to revamp marital and family relationships and thus build a better world. This, I believe, is the author's dream. It is certainly God's dream!

—Rev. Elisha Gaiya
Pastor, New Revelation Baptist Church
Ikeja, Lagos

This book is amazing! As a pastor in a large congregation, I gave this book to a troubled couple who had been married for four years and were having serious marital problems. I instructed them to read and discuss it. They came back grinning from ear to ear—they had made up! They said they have since read this wonderful book three times!

I recommend this book to all married couples even if they have no marital problems; it will encourage better understanding and communication in marriage.

—Pastor Jordan Bowman
Dominion Chapel, Abuja

The book *How to Love a Man Forever* is an inspirational book which was given to us by our own dear Aunty Bidemi in preparation towards our wedding and it has become a reference material to us…it has changed our thinking. This book has been a positive influence on our lives and we can honestly say, through what we have gathered from this book we are ready to make our marriage work and also face every challenge the marriage intends to have later (since no marriage is perfect)…Many thanks to the author, who through this book will save many marriages and guide those who intend to get married like us, which also means that this book is recommended to all, including singles because it will help guide your steps and also assist in making the right decision. God bless you.

—Olamide and Oluwasegun
Lagos, Nigeria

The wrong impression that marriages are not meant to last is being created and accepted due to the alarmingly high rate of marriage failures, even among Christians. Nevertheless, a proper understanding and management of marital relations can help make any marriage happy and lasting. Olapeju Otsemobor's book, *How to Love a*

HOW TO
LOVE A MAN
FOREVER

Olapeju Otsemobor

CREATION
HOUSE

Library of Congress Cataloging-in-Publication Data:
2012946651
International Standard Book Number: 978-1-62136-099-5
E-book International Standard Book Number:
978-1-62136-100-8

While the author has made every effort to provide accurate
telephone numbers and Internet addresses at the time of
publication, neither the publisher nor the author assumes
any responsibility for errors or for changes that occur after
publication.

First edition

12 13 14 15 16 — 9 8 7 6 5 4 3 2 1

Dedication

This book is dedicated to women of all ages and stations in life—especially the divas. A diva is a woman who is strong, confident, and comfortable in her own skin and can inspire others to feel the same way! Being a diva is about a woman's attitude, confidence, and greatness, even as she embraces her femininity. A diva doesn't run herself down and won't allow others to make her feel bad about who she is. She is able to leave her past hurts and pains in the past in order to live a more fulfilling life.

A diva recognizes her own greatness, so she does not need affirmation from others. She knows her talents and uses them to create a better life for herself, then for her family and others around her. She has the strength and endurance to

Being a diva is about a woman's attitude, confidence, and greatness, even as she embraces her femininity. A diva doesn't run herself down and won't allow others to make her feel bad about who she is. She is able to leave her past hurts and pains in the past in order to live a more fulfilling life.

A diva recognizes her own greatness, so she does not need affirmation from others. She knows her talents and uses them to create a better life for herself, then for her family and others around her. She has the strength and endurance to work in her best interest. She knows that if she truly wants something, she has to work hard to get it. She doesn't let others or self-doubt get in her way. She makes sure that she takes care of herself—spirit, soul, and body.

work in her best interest. She knows that if she truly wants something, she has to work hard to get it. She doesn't let others or self-doubt get in her way. She makes sure that she takes care of herself—spirit, soul, and body.

I have shared my idea of who a diva is so that we are of like mind as we take a journey through this book. It is my fervent prayer that this book will open your eyes to your God-given personhood, enable you to be the best you can be, and help your husband become the best he can become.

Women have touched the world in diverse ways, yet the most profound of them is in the family. When a nation trains its women to have a voice and to contribute, it helps itself develop in perpetuity. A woman takes pride of place in family life and development. Women, as do men, pass through different stages in their lives, and the world would be a better place for helping them prepare for each stage ahead of time. The issue of relationships, without doubt, is central to the ability of the woman to put in her best at any stage in life.

Women also find themselves in different classes at different times in their lives. Whatever class you find yourself as a woman, it is up to you to change it if you do not like it. Women have the capacity to change their situations or circumstances. From whatever position a woman occupies, she can exercise this power to change her family in line with the purpose of God. It is for this power to bring out the best in people and circumstances that we celebrate our women, and I urge all women to unleash this power to bring out the best in their husbands and families.

As many women as commit to doing this, I encourage to become better at it, to pass on a tradition of godly relationships to their children, and to leave a Christian legacy of personal improvement and service. I have no doubt in my heart that every woman can do this successfully!

Acknowledgments

I am grateful to so many people who have contributed in many ways to my life and to making this book possible. I am grateful to all the people I have used as role models and examples in this book; some I have mentioned by name, and others I have not but have related events in their lives that are invaluable to the purpose of this book, which is to challenge women to rise to the imperative task of building a better world by building better homes.

I am so grateful to all my pastor friends who have contributed in numerous ways to transforming inspiration and ideas into writing: Rev. (Dr.) Idowu Akintola, for his many insightful sermons and for writing the foreword to this book; Rev. Segun Olugbemi, for listening to and encouraging my innovative thoughts; Rev. Sam Oye and Rev. Nkem Okemiri; Rev. Babajide Olowodola, for prayerful insights; the indomitable Deacon John Dara, and other deacons of New Estate Baptist Church, Abuja, also known as International Fellowship Centre.

My thanks also go to Honourable Justice Olatokunbo

Olopade, Chief Judge of Ogun State, for allowing me to use her story; Mr. and Mrs. Oladejo Ajayi; Engineer Clement and Dr. Yetunde Oke, among so many others.

I thank my niece, Adekemi Kudehinbu, and the team of professionals who handled different aspects of this book to bring it to a high standard.

I want to thank my brothers and sisters for being the first to taste of my compulsion to make things better by obeying instructions at very tender ages. Each has gone on to make the best of their lives and relationships.

I thank all my in-laws—especially my mother-in-law, Mama Adiza Igbanoi—for being so accepting of me. I also thank the entire Orbih dynasty. My life is that much richer because of you all.

I thank the entire congregation of New Estate Baptist Church, Abuja, especially Shade Adepoju, for their support in diverse ways.

I thank my husband and children for their support at all times. Special thanks to our son, Osi, the multitalented creative artist in the family, for his many suggestions.

Above all, I thank God for using the power of the Holy Spirit not only to stir up the idea for this book, but also to compel me to write in spite of a crowded schedule. God is king, and He is awesome!

Contents

Part Three

Part Four

Part Five

Part Six

Foreword

In this generation, marriage and the home have been altered drastically. Our world is changing; because of these changes, our lifestyles are changing, and so are our marriages. Nowadays, men are afraid to be men, women are ashamed to be women, and children are confused about who is in charge. There are blended and not-so-well-blended families, and there are homes that have become battle grounds. Many marriages are so unstable and temporary.

Every generation needs a new revolution. We need a love revolution to address the attack on our homes, families, and love relationships. We need to overthrow selfishness and self-centeredness in our lives and relationships. Nothing will change in our world unless each one of us is willing to change.

How to Love a Man Forever, I believe, will bring about the change we all long for in our families and ignite a love revolution in every heart. We have tried many methods for addressing family crises; this book recommends God's remedy for solving every interpersonal issue: the love way. God is love! Love is and has always been God's idea. He came to love us and to teach us to love Him and ourselves and others. You can love your man forever.

I recommend this book by my beloved sister, woman of God, evangelist, deaconess, and crusader of righteousness to all in search of true joy and fruitfulness in their family lives. This book will ignite in you a love revolution.

Happy reading!

—Rev. Idowu Akintola, Senior Pastor
New Estate Baptist Church,
Abuja, Nigeria

Preface

In writing this book, I did not set out to look for a perfect marriage because that would have been a daunting task. Rather, I have looked for what has worked in the lives of various couples and drawn lessons from them. I have also drawn lessons from the things that did not work so we can avoid their pitfalls. In spite of the many incomplete manuscripts littering my laptop, I am not a writer—at least, not until now. As a result, I have written from the heart of a woman who wants to see marriages blossom and society improve as we learn lessons from those who have gone before us into this holy institution. We can build a better world, one marriage at a time.

I look forward to this book setting the agenda for revamping relationships and

We can build a better world, one marriage at a time.

marriages, generating ideas for improvement in family life and input for subsequent editions. Consequently, I would appreciate the use of this book for group discussions. Feel free to agree and disagree with parts of it and make helpful contributions to improve it.

As flawed as many marriages are, the institution remains very attractive. This is the reason some people never give up on marriage when their marriages fail; they keep getting in and out of marriages.

All who love God must contribute to repairing the frayed edges of this institution called marriage. I believe that God instituted marriage for man and that we need to go back to Him to make it work well. I am aware of the need to apply balance, and I will attempt, subsequently, to address issues that are important to the success of marriage from the male angle with some help from men themselves. I will start from the female angle so that charity, indeed, will start at home.

Part One

❧

One

The Reason for This Book

I HAD PLANNED TO write about "bigger" things, such as leadership, entrepreneurship, nation building, and global issues, and if I had followed that plan, a book of this kind would have taken the back seat on my list of books to write! I would probably have gotten to it in the long run, but only after I'd dealt with more pressing issues. The Lord began to challenge my thinking, though, and point out to me that the most effective path to nation building is through building effective families! All of those lofty things I wanted to do would be enhanced if families worked well and produced well-adjusted individuals. As I began to see the connection, I got more compelled to write this book, to the extent that I would wake up at night with

> Every time I see an opportunity to make things better, my heart stirs, and it was happening with this book.

3

ideas to include in it. Every time I see an opportunity to make things better, my heart stirs, and it was happening with this book.

If I may backtrack a little, almost two decades ago a dear Christian friend of mine had problems with her marriage and moved out of her matrimonial home. From her narration of the issues leading to this, the problems seemed intractable. We both commenced a series of prayer meetings to deal with the issues, and in one such meeting the Lord gave us a word of prophecy that she would return to her home. Knowing how grave the situation was, I was embarrassed by this prophecy because it seemed most unlikely to come to pass, since another woman had already moved into her husband's house. Nevertheless, since the Lord had said it, we continued to pray.

I did a bit of counseling with my friend and decided to meet her husband. Tentatively, he listened to me and told me he had already started making plans to divorce his wife. Then he stopped and said he had read in the Bible that God hates divorce (Mal. 2:16) and that was giving him some doubts. I knew the Lord had started a work of reconciliation in his heart, so I was greatly encouraged to continue counseling with my friend. By divine orchestration, the strange woman was flushed out and the couple was reunited. They are now grandparents!

The battle against the family is fierce, many-sided, and unrelenting. There is no stage at which the devil cannot attack a marriage, and no level of spirituality exempts a marriage from being attacked. We need to keep learning, planning, and praying for the success of our marriages.

Every woman must be a spiritual and physical gatekeeper

for her home to prevent the entry of diverse problems. We must confront and overwhelm every challenge through the power of God. Every woman who reads this book must commit to going into marriage without the "way of escape" mentality. The "way of escape" mentality harbors such thoughts as, "I will give this marriage a trial; if it doesn't work, I will quickly opt out." Women who think like this have scant regard for the institution of marriage and have no commitment to make it work. If you are one such person, please change this attitude before you get married or, better still, do so right now.

When you commit to a marriage, you give God a chance to help you make it work. It means you are willing to become a partner with God, to walk in line with His purpose. You will also help society by reducing the number of broken or unstable families in our space—that is, our state, country, and the kingdom of God. Nation building may become a little easier as we raise better-adjusted citizens.

Marriage is possibly one of the most important institutions that people go into without adequate preparation. There are schools for almost every endeavor you may wish to engage in, but there are no schools to prepare a person for marriage. Some people believe that marriage is a school and that one has to get married before one can enroll and learn the rudiments of it. I want to challenge that proposition and suggest that each family should prepare its children (both male and female) for marriage.

Women usually ask their daughters to take part in kitchen chores in an attempt to prepare them for marriage but then leave the boys to go and play football. Cooking is good, but it is just one of so many things that our daughters need to learn in preparation for marriage. As for boys, they are hardly taught anything other than that each of them will be the head of his family and can lord it over his wife as he deems fit. This mentality has caused more pain than pleasure in many marriages, as decisions are usually taken at the whim of the man or the wile of the woman.

The church has risen stoutly to address this issue of preparing young people for marriage through pre-marriage counseling, and we need concerted effort to ensure that both males and females are adequately prepared for marriage. I will, in another book, attempt to address the men's contributions toward a good marriage.

Now, in some societies, as a wedding ceremony is being performed, outside the church there are lawyers standing in the wings to give the couple complimentary cards, just in case they require an attorney to handle their divorce! Marriages are not even given a chance to survive. This is partly due to the already high rate of divorce and broken marriages, some of which lead to broken lives. Also, in some societies, an elaborate divorce ritual takes place where the marriage ring is cracked and the relationship broken symbolically. The couple then separate with a celebration and are still regarded as friends. This is rather difficult to understand—celebrating the separation from a person you were once so attracted to and decided to marry in order to make your relationship permanent!

Statistics on divorce are not readily available in Africa, yet where available, they are alarming and embarrassing.

I went to many courts in Abuja, Nigeria, searching for information on marriages and divorces. Getting access to data was a Herculean task due to poor record keeping. At one of the courts, a lawyer I spoke with was rather excited and asked me if I already had an attorney or was looking for one. He thought I wanted to file for a divorce!

I was able to get some incomplete data on the number of petitions for divorce filed in FCT high court. As incomplete as it is, it is indicative of the growing problem of failing marriages in Nigeria. Between May and December 2009, the court had registered 104 petitions for divorce. In 2010, the court registered 185, while between January and November 2011, it had registered 244 cases.[1]

Some divorce cases seem extreme; for instance, a mere 72 days after their lavish televised wedding, broadcast to over 2 million viewers, two Hollywood stars, Kim Kardashian and Kris Humphries, got a divorce.[2] Some divorces arise from unspoken expectations on the part of the man or woman; one woman wanted to divorce her husband because he wanted her to cut down on her celebrity outings and settle down to a married life. One would have expected that a woman who went into marriage was ready to "settle down"!

The world has made profound advances in science and technology but so little in the issue of relationships. According to an online divorce magazine, in the United States, 49 percent of marriages end in divorce.[3] Each 100 additional divorces worldwide will lead to two additional suicides, one additional murder, 6 additional rapes, 33 additional armed robberies, and puts another 100 men in prison.[4]

The Christian home is not spared, as we probably know one or two marriages among Christians that have ended in separation, divorce, and a lot of bitterness. This is a clarion call to let us know that we must do more to improve the outcomes in our marriages and, in turn, prevent the attendant sorrow and pain they unleash on society if they break down.

What Happened?

Where did women get it wrong? Carol T. Mowbray, in her book, *Women and Health: New Directions for Change*, observed that marriage seems to have a "protective" effect on men but a negative effect on women. According to her, married men have significantly fewer *mental* health *problems*, while *married women* have more *problems* than either single women or single men.[5]

In my research for this book, I came across a funny but somewhat true comparison between men and women entitled "Why Men Are Seldom Depressed." Due to its length, I am unable to reproduce the entire piece here, but this excerpt will suffice:

> Men Are Just Happier People
> What do you expect from such simple creatures?
> Your last name stays put.
> You can never be pregnant.
> You can wear a white T-shirt to a water park.
> You can wear no shirt to a water park.
> Car mechanics tell you the truth.
> Same work, more pay.

Wrinkles add character.

Wedding dress $5000. Tux rental-$100.

People never stare at your chest when you're talking to them.

One mood all the time.

Phone conversations are over in 30 seconds flat.

A five-day vacation requires only one suitcase.

You get extra credit for the slightest act of thoughtfulness.

On money, a man will pay $2 for a $1 item he needs.

A woman will pay $1 for a $2 item that she doesn't need but it's on sale.

A man has six items in his bathroom: toothbrush and toothpaste, shaving cream, razor, a bar of soap, and a towel.

The average number of items in the typical woman's bathroom is 337. A man would not be able to identify more than 20 of these items.

A woman has the last word in any argument. Anything a man says after that is the beginning of a new argument.

A woman worries about the future until she gets a husband.

A man never worries about the future until he gets a wife.

A woman marries a man expecting he will change, but he doesn't.

> A man marries a woman expecting that she won't change, but she does.
>
> A married man should forget his mistakes. There's no use in two people remembering the same thing![6]

These wisecracks may be true sometimes, but they form a stereotype that women need to overcome. Women have come a long way, but there is still so much left to do to enable us to enjoy womanhood without comparing ourselves to men or pulling each other down. If well-managed, the effects of these differences between men and women on the success of our marriages can be less stressful and disruptive.

Kevin Miller, in his article entitled "Two Keys to a Happy Marriage," noted that:

> Almost every marriage starts out as a huge celebration. Together with their family and friends, each couple is full of hopes and dreams for their future life together. But the road to a happy marriage is far from easy. And as today's divorce statistics demonstrate all too well, many couples opt not to complete the journey.[7]

Another article I found by a writer that resonates with me has been included below. It is entitled "Characteristics of a Good Woman":

> A good woman is proud of herself, she respects herself and others. She is aware

of who she is. She neither seeks definition from the person she is with, nor does she expect them to read her mind. She is quite capable of articulating her needs.

A good woman is hopeful. She is strong enough to make all her dreams come true. She knows love; therefore, she gives love. She recognizes that her love has great value and must be reciprocated. If her love is taken for granted, it soon disappears.

A good woman has a dash of inspiration, a dabble of endurance. She knows that she will, at times, have to inspire others to reach the potential God gave them.

A good woman knows her past, understands her present, and moves toward the future.

A good woman knows God. She knows that with God, the world is her playground, but without God, she will just be played.

A good woman does not live in fear of the future because of her past. Instead, she understands that her life experiences are merely lessons, meant to bring her closer to self-knowledge and unconditional self-love.

Girl, smile. You know you have it going on! So keep on keeping on.[8]

Two

What to Do Before "I Do"?

THIS BOOK IS primarily for those who have made the decision to get married or are already married, but I have added this chapter because some single ladies might find it helpful. Remember, therefore, whatever you want others to do to you, do so unto them (Matt. 7:12, author's paraphrase).

Why do you want to get married? Is it because you have reached the right age, or because you want to prevent a stream of male suitors from distracting you? Is it because your parents are anxious to have you married and give them grandchildren? Perhaps you have met an irresistible gentleman that you think is worth the effort. The list could be quite long, but you have to be clear in your mind what your major reasons are.

> Remember, therefore, whatever you want others to do to you, do so unto them (Matt. 7:12, author's paraphrase).

What positive traits would you bring into your proposed marriage? When you have clarified these, you need to take a look at your character and decide what needs to change for you to make a success of marriage. Please, be brutally frank with yourself. If you have a trusted girlfriend, you could assist each other in identifying character traits you have and what may need to be changed.

Are you a confident, responsible, emotionally stable adult who is able to handle the responsibilities of a relationship? What are your expectations from the man you plan to marry? What is the difference between your expectations and the traits you can observe in the man you plan to marry? Bearing in mind your findings, are you willing to continue with the relationship? Prayerfully make your choice, and do not string along any man only to dump him when you find what you consider a better man. If a relationship is not likely to work, give it up instead of waiting for replacement or orchestrating a quarrel. This may be difficult, but the earlier the relationship is done away with, the better for you both.

How Are You Searching for the Right Man?

There are no hard and fast rules for searching for the right spouse, but every woman must be decent and dignified in relating romantically with men.

Do you ogle every man you see, wondering if he is the right man, or are you so tense that any man who says hello has your heart racing and you start to wonder whether he has a proposition coming? Relax, girl. Enjoy yourself, develop yourself, pray, and find the man within your heart.

You always need to prayerfully confirm every sweet

word, every promise, and every decision in the course of this phase of your life. Life is literally at your feet—and there are so many opportunities, divas. Don't blow them! Don't allow anyone to demean you by attacking your sense of self-worth—God gave it to you!

If you are a Christian and reading this book, I urge you by the mercies of God: Do not commit yourself to marrying a man who does not share your faith in the lordship of Jesus Christ and the Christian heritage you have. There are too many women regretting such decisions. In such marriages, the husband may prevent his wife from going to church or taking their children to church with her. Worse still, he may insist that she convert to his religion or way of worship. This will lead to heartache for her if she has walked closely with the Lord. Even when a man assures you before the marriage that serving God is a personal issue and he will respect your faith, do not be deceived into believing this ploy to get you into marriage. Remember, it is in your interest to make decisions that are in line with who you are, not decisions that will transform you into another person, one who is unable to enjoy life and fulfill God's purpose for her life.

Arlene Harder, in an article on unspoken expectations of people who go into marriage, says that many of the conflicts that arise later in relationships are as a result of these unspoken contracts between spouses. She emphasized some important things to look out for, some of which are:

- Open and clear communication
- Important intellectual differences between the partners

- Significant differences in the level of energy each person brings into the relationship (for example, intensity and enthusiasm)
- Major differences of opinion and outlook
- Level of comfort in dealing with each other's families
- The money-power dynamic in the relationship (that is, if the power in the relationship lies with the partner who provides financially)
- The sharing of domestic tasks and chores (do both parties contribute in this area, or does one person feel overburdened?)
- How well a couple's core values—such as religion, politics, ethics, and so on—align.[1]

The list can be much longer, depending on the couple. What is important is the fact that each person in a relationship has expectations that, if not discussed, may cause disagreements or disappointment in their marriage.

Inability to resolve conflicts is also a potent force in breaking up marriages. Of course, we all know how difficult it can be to admit when we are wrong or that we contribute to the problems in our marriages. As a result, the unwillingness of each partner to take responsibility for their part in creating the problems is at the heart of the inability of most couples to resolve conflict. Certainly, we need to learn effective communication and conflict resolution skills, both of which are very important. We women also need to learn to be sincere and to accept that we are as imperfect as our husbands.

A Word for the Wise!

When a man tells you, "I married the wrong woman," it is another way of his saying you are the right woman! Girl, give him a wide berth. He is a distracted man looking for a toy and will only complicate your life. Do not encourage him by giving him kindness or a listening ear. Send him back to his wife and let them sort out their issues. All the stories he might feed you with, describing his wife as a bad woman, are just a ploy to get you into bed. If they are still living together, he probably is still sleeping with this "wrong woman," and there are many more things binding them together than you will ever know. Do not facilitate any man's infidelity or transition to a divorce. It is not your place to wait in the wings for a man to divorce his wife so he can marry you. Do not make yourself a part of a tragic trio.

Another thing you may want to learn is that once a man starts changing wives, there will be no end to it; there will always be more lovely women for a man who is inclined to cheat. It is safe—wise, even—to assume that such a man is just physically attracted to you or is going through a rough patch in his marriage. There is an African adage that says that the stick a man used to beat his first wife is safely kept so it can be used for subsequent wives. Just send him home—to his wife—without bothering to learn the details.

If you believe these sorts of things do not happen to the Christian girl, think again. Christian girls are under a lot of assault from many quarters, and a few of them have gone on to make very poor choices in marriage partners.

Prepare!

Once a definite decision has been made to get married, start to spiritually, physically, emotionally, and financially prepare for your marriage so nothing is left unattended.

Three

The Great Christian Heritage

THE FAMILY IS at the heart of God's plan and purpose for the world. Therefore, all people committed to God must work for the health of this institution. John Dara, a contemporary preacher and man of God, said: "The family is ordained by God, modelled after the Holy Trinity, demonstrated by the relationship between Jesus Christ and the church, practiced by Joseph the carpenter, and made workable by the continual presence of God through the Holy Spirit. The Trinity is united, holy, powerful, loving, and has a great heritage."

This can be applied to the Christian family, which is expected to be united, holy, powerful, loving, and has a great heritage to pass on to succeeding generations. Our commitment to

> "The family is ordained by God, modelled after the Holy Trinity, demonstrated by the relationship between Jesus Christ and the church, practiced by Joseph the carpenter, and made workable by the continual presence of God through the Holy Spirit. The Trinity is

united, holy, powerful, loving, and has a great heritage."

encouraging better marriages is central to this great heritage of the Christian. Marriage as an institution would have ceased to exist by now, as a result of the continuing assault on it, if it were not God-ordained. The devil has worked against the family from the beginning in the Garden of Eden. Genesis 3:1–7 details an account of the encounter between the devil on one side and Adam and Eve on the other. Any good Bible reader would come to the understanding that Eve was not alone but had only acted as the spokesperson for the family:

> The serpent was the craftiest of all the creatures the Lord God had made. So the serpent came to the woman. "Really?" he asked. "None of the fruit in the garden? God says you mustn't eat any of it?"
>
> "Of course we may eat it," the woman told him. "It's only the fruit in the middle of the garden that we are not to eat. God says we mustn't eat it, or even touch it, or we will die."
>
> "That's a lie!" the serpent

hissed. "You'll not die! God knows very well that the instant you eat it you will become like him, for your eyes will be opened—you will be able to distinguish good from evil!"

The woman was convinced. How lovely and fresh looking it was! And it would make her wise! So she ate some of the fruit and gave some to her husband and he ate it too.

And as they ate it, suddenly they became aware of their nakedness and were embarrassed. So they strung fig leaves together to cover themselves around the hips.

—Genesis 3:1–7

From the fall of man until the birth of the Lord Jesus Christ, men and women in diverse milieu have tried in various ways to restore the institution of marriage. They recorded limited success until the coming of Jesus Christ, who clarified major issues concerning marriage. It was the Lord Jesus, for example, who made us realize that marriage is supposed to be permanent until death. In Mark 10:11–12 Jesus said: "When a man divorces his wife to marry someone else, he commits adultery against her. And if a wife divorces her husband and remarries, she too commits adultery."

He also explained the need for a man to leave his father and mother and cleave to his wife. Mark 10:6–9 (KJV) says:

> But from the beginning of creation God made them male and female. For this cause

shall a man leave his father and mother, and cleave to his wife; and the twain shall be one flesh. What therefore God hath joined together, let not man put asunder.

These teachings of the Lord improved the estimation of women in the eyes of all, as against what worth women had been ascribed before Jesus walked the earth. This is enough reason for a woman to be confident and become who God called her to be. A confident woman is not in competition with her husband because she knows she is in a partnership and they both work for the interest of the family. She also knows that in a family, the husband is the head, just as in every team there is a leader. She is not a disadvantaged or weaker person fighting for emancipation or a unionist stalking her employer in order to get a better deal! The confident knowledge that women are vessels in the hands of God is important to the success of men, mankind, and civilization as we know it. It is in the interest of every godly woman to internalize these eternal principles and live by them.

Four

In the Beginning...

G OD MADE THE heavens and the earth and all that man needs for survival before He made man. God made woman out of man, thus ensuring that man is not complete without a woman. Together, they form a complete unit. And since women are not in competition with their husbands, they are to support and collaborate with them. Our husbands' success is our success, his challenges our challenges, his failures our failures, and we must ensure that they are successful in their faith, professions, and vocations.

Many women have read the book *The Power of a Praying Wife*, by Stormie Omartian, in which she set out the premise for praying thus:

> First of all, let me make it perfectly clear that the power of a praying wife is not a means of gaining control over her husband, so don't get your hopes up! In fact, it is just the opposite. It's laying down all

> No man with a Christian wife should be a failure in life. This is because women have a special place in the heart of God and can move His heart and hands to do great things! It is an overcoming woman that can love a man and develop a stable relationship, and a whole woman can love a man forever.

claim to power in and of yourself and relying on God's power to transform you, your husband, your circumstances, and your marriage.[1]

We must stand in the place of prayer for our husbands and families. No man with a Christian wife should be a failure in life. This is because women have a special place in the heart of God and can move His heart and hands to do great things! It is an overcoming woman that can love a man and develop a stable relationship, and a whole woman can love a man forever. An overcoming woman, I believe, is one committed to a relationship with God through the Lord Jesus Christ. By being whole, I mean a woman who is mature and has a sense of responsibility and commitment to her relationships. We need these two attributes to make any marriage stable and successful. No woman (or indeed man) can give what she does not have. This book is an attempt to help every woman become an overcomer as a first step to becoming whole. When this happens, she is ready and able to enrich the lives of her husband, children, and people around her and, by ripple effect, can influence the whole world! Developing a wholesome attitude in life is something everyone should work toward, but we emphasize women in this book because a woman's role is pivotal to the success of the family.

Part Two

❧

Five

The Purpose of Marriage

IT HAS BEEN said that if the purpose of a thing is not known, it will be abused. It is important that every woman who goes into marriage does so with a full knowledge of the purpose of marriage according to God's Word.

After God made woman from man and commanded them to multiply and fill and subdue the earth, He further gave them dominion (power and authority) over the created animals and plants (Gen. 1:27–30). Some of God's purposes for marriage, as stated in the Bible, are companionship (Gen. 2:18), procreation (Gen. 1:28), mutual and undefiled pleasure (1 Cor. 7:4–5; Prov. 5:18–19; Song of Solomon; Heb. 13:4), prevention of immorality (1 Cor. 7:2, 5), the serving of Christ as a whole and properly representing the

It is good breeding to be a virtuous woman, and this is not in conflict with being a modern and confident woman.

spiritual relationship between Christ and the church (Eph. 5:22–33), and the raising of godly descendants (Mal. 2:13–16). The bond of marriage (when respected) leads to the good of not only the couple and their children, but also that of the society as a whole, for the family unit is the building block of any society.

God wants the team of man and woman to multiply and administer the world on His behalf. This means that every woman is to form a team, or partnership, with her husband and take charge of some aspects of living on the earth on behalf of God. You may call this aspect your profession, vocation, or any other way you choose to describe it. There is yet a lot to learn about our roles in dominating the earth, and it is as we improve our relationships that we reach a better understanding of this.

When the man and woman are not working in unity, they are like a house divided against itself, which cannot stand. Matthew 12:25 says: "Jesus knew their thoughts and replied, 'A divided kingdom ends in ruin. A city or home divided against itself cannot stand.'" If the couple, as a team, must administer the earth on behalf of God, they must know their part in this work and must be accountable to God.

Marriage is also for companionship so that man should not be alone. Loneliness remains a major problem among many humans, and everyone needs a close relationship to prevent it. Two are better than one (Eccl. 4:9–11). The absence of a reliable companion (a spouse, for example) can be associated with emotional problems such as anxiety, desolation, and insecurity.

Marriage was also created to populate the earth with

godly children who will serve God's purpose. Marriage is important to God in replenishing the earth and for fellowship. We Christian women are God's agents for increasing His influence in the world. When we get married, we commit ourselves to populating the earth with children dedicated to God and brought up in His ways; we stand on the side of God in the battle between good and evil. We are aware that Satan is a created being that stands for evil and is against God, but he cannot be equal to God. It is the godly woman who can best demonstrate this stance by raising godly children in a wicked and dying world. The word of life must be bequeathed to our children in a way that will help them to compete favorably in the world and serve God in their generation. We must entrust to them our unwavering faith in God and demonstrate the qualities of the virtuous woman even in a modern world. It is good breeding to be a virtuous woman, and this is not in conflict with being a modern and confident woman.

Every woman who gets married and raises a family is privileged to mold the life of another person. This is a privilege women must not scorn or treat lightly. I believe an understanding of this important function will disabuse many women's minds from the injustice they undergo in relationships due to perceived inferiority. You are complementary to your husband and bring to your relationship what he cannot bring. While babies are in the womb, we must begin to speak the Word of God to them and transfer godliness to them. As soon as our babies are born, we begin to read the Word of God to them and dedicate them to God, even before they are brought to church for formal dedication. We must lead our children to declare faith in the Lord Jesus Christ as soon as they can understand the Gospel's message. The faith that was committed to us must be transferred to our children as part of our service to God.

Godly Women in Warfare

Stacy Wiebe, in her touching article, "The Power of a Mother's Promise," said:

> Twenty-seven years ago this month, my mom made a promise that changed our lives forever. Now that I'm also a mother, I've come to see that promise as a kind of spiritual umbilical cord, a maternal link God used to bring new life to me and my family, and to countless others.[1]

We shall spend some time discussing prayer, since it is the major way we reach God. Many godly women continue to have problems with their children as a result of carelessness. Some of these children fall into bad company, and the spirit of the world takes over their lives. This is partly due to parents' ignorance of the wiles of the devil and poor understanding of the resources that are available to the Christian woman in prayer warfare.

Prayer is communication with God by sincere conversation. Through prayer, we experience a relationship with God; therefore, the quality of our prayer life determines the quality of our relationship with God. Prayer is talking with God, listening to God, and enjoying the presence of God. It can take many forms:

worship, confession, thanksgiving, praise, petition (asking for things), waiting (silence, listening and sensing God), and warfare (command). If we are baptized in the Spirit, we can pray in tongues, in languages unknown to us but known to God (1 Cor. 14:2, 14). You don't have to be a preacher to pray to God. All you really have to do is open your mouth and speak to Him, as if you were speaking to anyone else. Ask the Holy Spirit to be an intercessor for you in prayer. In prayer, God is looking for a heartfelt relationship.

The power of prayer should not be underestimated. James 5:16–18 declares:

> The prayer of a righteous man has great power and wonderful results.
>
> Elijah was completely human as we are, and yet when he prayed earnestly that no rain would fall, none fell for the next three and one half years. Then he prayed again, that this time it would rain, and down it poured and the grass turned green and the gardens began to grow again.

God most definitely listens to and answers prayers. Jesus taught, "For if you have faith as small as a tiny mustard seed, you could say to this mountain, 'Move!' and it would go far away. Nothing will be impossible" (Matt. 17:20).

Also, 2 Corinthians 10:4–5 tells us, "The weapons we fight with are not the weapons of the world. On the contrary, they have divine power to demolish strongholds. We demolish arguments and every pretension that sets itself up against the knowledge of God, and we take captive every thought to make it obedient to Christ." The Bible urges us, "And pray in the Spirit on all occasions with all kinds of prayers and requests. With this in mind, be alert and always keep on praying for all the saints" (Eph. 6:18).

You can tap into the power of prayer just by praying to God. The power of prayer does not lie in the person praying; it resides in the God who is being prayed to. 1 John 5:14–15 tells us, "This is the confidence we have in approaching God: that if we ask anything according to his will, he hears us. And if we know that he hears us— whatever we ask—we know that we have what we asked of him." It does not matter who the person praying is, the passion behind the prayer, or the purpose of the prayer; God answers prayers that are in agreement with His will. His answers are not always yes but are always in our best interests. When our desires line up with His will, we will come to understand this. When we pray passionately and purposefully, according to God's will, God responds powerfully! God's help, through the power of prayer, is available for all kinds of requests and issues.

Philippians 4:6–7 tells us, "Do not be anxious about anything, but in everything, by prayer and petition, with thanksgiving, present your requests to God. And the peace of God, which transcends all understanding, will guard your hearts and your minds in Christ Jesus." Praying the Word of God through his Scriptures is always a good place to start.

As mentioned before, there are different forms of

prayer. The Holy Spirit wants to lead us into a balance of all these kinds of prayer.

Worship

In true worship, there is a total bowing of the heart to God. In worship, we express love and admiration for God, which is a response to the revelation, by the Holy Spirit, of who God is. Worship is voluntary submission to the love, will, and law of God. Any hypocrisy disqualifies us from true worship. In worship, we hear the voice of God.

Confession

In confession of sins, we tell God our sins with our mouths. We should specifically tell God what wrong we did or acknowledge what we failed to do that we should have done. This is necessary to restore communion with God and is a preparation for further fellowship. In confession of the Word, we tell God with our mouths what He has said in His Word. We express faith and confidence in God and His Word verbally, and it releases the blessing of God upon us. Very rarely do we rise above the level of our verbal confession before God.

Thanksgiving

Thanksgiving is thanking God for what He has done for us. We can thank Him both for blessings seen and those as yet unseen. Thanksgiving is a key to faith, and it is natural and right that we give thanks always to the One from whom all good things come (1 Thess. 5:18).

Praise

Praise is declaring good things about God, both about His character (who He is) and His actions. To say, "God is good," for instance, is to praise God. There are many styles of praise. Some are noisy and exuberant, others are calm. Praise is well-expressed through music, singing, words, shouting, clapping, dancing, and giving to God.

Petition

Petition means asking God for the things we desire. Jesus said, "Ask and you shall receive" (Matt. 7:7). We are commanded to ask. As we ask and receive answers to our prayers, our faith grows and we are emboldened to become better at the things we do both in our family life and other relationships.

Intercession

The ministry of intercession involves all the other types of prayer. However, the emphasis of the prayer ministry in intercession is the needs of others and the advancement of God's interests in the world. It is not focused on praying for oneself.

Waiting (Habakkuk 2:1)

Waiting is a form of prayer in which the soul is silent and waits for God to move it or speak something by His Spirit. God promises to renew the strength of those who wait on Him (Isa. 40:31; Ps. 27:14). We are to wait patiently on God. Through this, we express to God in a practical way,

"Not my will but Yours be done." If we are always talking in prayer, we will not be able to hear what God is saying.

Warfare (Psalm 149:6-9)

Warfare is prayer directed against the powers of darkness (demons or fallen angels who are at work in the affairs of the world and the church). Our praises to God are also a weapon against them. We pronounce the written Word of God by reading the Scriptures of judgment against them (Ps. 149:9). We command them to be bound or to leave their positions of influence or authority in the name of Jesus (Matt. 16:19; Mark 16:17). In praying for the sick, we should pray prayers of command, ordering the bodies of people to be healed in Jesus' name. This is a form of spiritual warfare since it involves destroying the works of the devil (1 John 3:8; Acts 10:38).

Praying in Tongues
(1 Corinthians 14:2, 15; Jude 20)

Praying in tongues is a method of prayer available to those baptized in the Holy Spirit, through which they can pray the will of God through words given by the Spirit.

Praying the Word

Praying the Word, in a strict sense, includes quoting Scripture and using it in our prayers. God responds to His own Word; it will not return to Him void (Isa. 55:11). We can take general promises from the Bible and, using the words of Scripture, pray as if we expect that God will fulfill them for us personally. This is a powerful form of prayer.

Prayer warfare is a major topic on its own and cannot be discussed fully here. However, I wish to suggest that issues of allegiances to other persons before you met your spouse, covenants taken on your behalf by your parents, and vows made to other deities before you were born be dealt with in each family as soon as a man and woman get married, even before the children are born. A brief mention of these forms of relational contracts will be discussed later in this book. Every woman must be a prayer warrior and stand in the place of prayer for her family.

Bathe Your Husband in Prayer

This could mean the difference between life and death, success and failure, good judgment and error, optimism and pessimism, courage and fear, victory and failure when tempted to do wrong, and, above all, love and hate. This is an elaborate call to prayer, as no aspect of your husband's life should be exempt from your prayers. I know a godly woman whose husband ran into a serious problem that led to his suspension from the Federal Civil Service. His wife literally prayed heaven down into the matter until he was reinstated. Such is the fervency I am calling for in the life of every woman.

Your relationship with God may have become frosty due to misuse or disuse. You may need to deal with some issues in order to stand in the place of prayer for your husband. This will help you become an example to the women who need to embrace God and contribute to a better society.

Establish an Altar

If your husband has not done this already, establish an altar in your home. There should be a prayer time for the family at least once a day. Encourage your husband to participate and lead the prayer, and keep on encouraging him until he becomes comfortable with it. A home that has no altar to the Lord Jesus will have an altar to any other god. There is no home that does not worship a god; the question is, which god are they worshipping? The god they worship may even be unknown to the family, but it answers for them and will keep their allegiance, even if this allegiance came through generational relationships along their family lines. This book has a different theme and therefore cannot go into detail on this important topic.

The Woman in Procreation

The woman is an agent of God in creating a better world. The Bible says that God made the heavens and earth and everything in them and completed His work of creation in six days: "Now at last the heavens and earth were successfully completed, with all they contained. So on the seventh day, having finished his task, God ceased from this work he had been doing" (Gen. 2:1–2).

Marriage is the union of a man and a woman, creating a new entity, a new "whole" (one flesh). This union is brought about by a mutual commitment before God (expressed usually through a public vow) to forsake all others, keep themselves only unto their new partner, act in the best interest of the other (to love), and seek to fulfill God's purposes for their lives as a new unit. This commitment is to last as long as they both live (1 Cor. 7:39).

Marriage is not merely a friendship. Although it is not consummation that signals the beginning of a marriage (or Joseph and Mary would not have been married until after Christ was born—Matthew 1:25), sexual activity is understood to be a natural part of marriage (Ex. 21:10; Heb. 13:4). Today, the exchanging of the vows during a wedding ceremony is the vocalization of the commitment that was understood between biblical couples such as Isaac and Rebecca in Genesis 24:67.

As far as human life is concerned, both men and women have been given the power to procreate, but women are strategic to the fulfillment of this power. The woman nurtures a baby in the womb right from conception until birth. After delivery, the woman nurtures the baby until it is able to take care of itself. The woman is, thus, a nurturer and continues to nurture members of the family. This ability to nurture is important in the fulfillment of God's purpose for the family and the nations of the world. A woman has the privilege of being in partnership with God for the fulfillment of His purpose. It is a woman's duty to make a success of this calling in the lives of all members of her family. This requires prayer, planning, and a lifetime commitment.

Any bad trait prevalent in society presents a challenge to the woman to wield a stronger influence over her children. If society does not respect women, it is as a result of poor parenting, and there is need to challenge women on this issue.

For Emotional Needs and to Prevent Sexual Sins

When a man and woman marry, they consent to keep themselves to each other. A woman must be presentable and remain desirable to her husband.

God has endowed women with the capability to attract the opposite sex, and this must be used to the maximum in marriage. Sexual power is one of the strongest forces a person possesses, and it can be use positively or negatively. A woman must commit to the positive use of sex in marriage. A woman must satisfy the sexual needs of her husband. Because of the Bible's commandment to be chaste before marriage, this may require some time and practice but should not constitute any big problem.

Sex has become a weapon in the hands of the devil for destroying people and the institution of marriage. Every woman must help her husband keep the marriage vow and not fall into temptation. Infidelity in marriage has reached an alarming point, and even Christians are not spared. It is time women rose to deal with this issue. Having said this, I must add that the final responsibility for a person's action lies with that person.

Six

The Eve in You

PROVERBIAL PHILOSOPHY HAS long agreed that the woman is a complex creature, little understood, and there are many descriptions for her: "She is a miracle of divine contradictions"; "Woman's at best a contradiction still"; "A woman is the most inconsistent compound of obstinacy and self-sacrifice that I am acquainted with." The wisest sages from the earliest periods in time have been forced to admit that he would be a truly clever man who could understand, and account for, the many and varied characteristics of womankind.

Lord Byron wrote:

> What a strange thing is
> man! And what a stranger

Zig Ziglar said, "When you talk, you only say what you already know; when you listen, you learn what someone else knows."

Is woman! What a whirlwind is her head!
And what a whirlpool, full of depth and
danger,
Is all the rest about her! Whether wed
Or widow, maid or mother, she can
change her
Mind like the wind; whatever she has said
Or done, is light to what she shall say or do
The oldest thing on record, and yet new.[1]

And yet it is universally acknowledged that the woman is indispensable to man's happiness and well-being, for, as the German adage says, "Man without woman is head without body, woman without man is body without head."

According to another of their proverbial maxims, "Her intelligence is four times that of man, her assiduity six times, and her desires eight times." Here are some Eastern proverbs that compliment women: "Women are instructed by nature; the learning of men is taught by books." "Nature is the woman's teacher, and she learns more sense than man, the pedant, gleans from books."

The power and influence of the woman have been described through time and history. On the other hand, she has had her fair share discrimination and recrimination. A Spanish maxim says, "A woman's counsel is not much, but he that despises it is a fool." Consider these French proverbs: "Women can do everything, because they rule those who command everything." "Women are the extreme; they are either better or worse than men." "The world is the book of women."

Women have often been said to be capable of handling

any emergency. A German saying expressed this idea this way: "Though an elephant and a tiger come, she will leap over them."

To present a side different from the old and contemporary views, a young man, in an article on women, lists five admirable characteristics of strong women as *intelligence, honesty, ambition, passion, and the ability to make up their minds.* This contemporary man must have a lot of respect for women, and more women must live up to this high expectation.

Having looked at old and modern perspectives on women, we can now move on to improving our relationships, especially with our husbands.

Learn to Listen

Women tend to be more talkative than men, so we need to balance this trait with the ability to listen. Practice the art of listening. The popular author Zig Ziglar said, "When you talk, you only say what you already know; when you listen, you learn what someone else knows." First and foremost, listen—not only with your ears, but even more so with your heart. We need to hear what other people are really saying, not just what we think they are saying. We need to listen to their feelings. Good communication and conflict resolution requires listening beyond the other person's words to their sometimes deep emotions and unspoken needs or wishes.

Careful listening ensures that we do not distort what the other person is trying to say. This is necessary because we each tend to interpret messages through our own perspectives. For example, if we are extremely sensitive

45

to criticism, we may interpret our husband's potentially helpful suggestion as a criticism.

As you talk less and listen more, you discover what others know that you may need to learn. You may also discover that others have problems you can help solve or introduce a helpful perspective. Since women are often good at empathizing, a new aspect of your life may evolve from listening and showing empathy. This will tremendously enrich your life and relationships. This poem readily comes to mind:

> Do more than hear, listen;
> Do more than agree, cooperate;
> Do more than work, excel;
> Do more than receive, release;
> Do more than read, apply;
> Do more than live, love.
>
> —Anonymous

Manage Your Vulnerability

Let's face it: Every woman becomes vulnerable as she falls in love and gets married. Managing this vulnerability is a challenge women must face. The choice of a spouse will have significant effects on your life spiritually, physically, and emotionally. If a wife is everything to everyone, juggling all parts while her husband looks on without lifting a hand to help her, he may soon have nothing left to enjoy in her. She would be totally spent! The lesson here is that husbands need to help their wives be their best as they cope with domestic issues and the demands of their careers. Wives also must be there for their husbands as they face their own issues in their careers or other relationships.

As a woman, you must have noticed that you cannot be all that is written in Proverbs 31 at every period of your life. The qualities of the virtuous woman in Proverbs 31 cover different stages in the woman's life; it is a panoramic view of the life of a godly woman. The strategic import of it is that the woman, with the help of her husband, looks after the needs of the family through the different stages of life.

For example, a newly married couple wants to spend plenty of time together, so the wife cannot afford to work late into the night, as is said of the virtuous woman in Proverbs 31:17. She has to look after her new family. To enable a wife perform well, a good understanding of the different stages in a marriage is important for the couple, especially the woman. It will afford her the opportunity to enjoy every stage of her life and marriage. A woman must learn to enjoy her marriage by preparing ahead of time.

Dear woman, if your husband provides everything in the family, from decisions to diapers, beware; you may soon have nothing left to enjoy in him, as he will be drained of life's vitality while seeking more and more wealth to satisfy you and time to generate all the decisions for the family. The lesson for the woman here is this: Help your husband be his best; don't facilitate an early grave for him! A mind on autopilot is hardly helpful to the family, especially in the competitive world of today. Husbands and wives must contribute to moving the family forward in an atmosphere of love and unity.

Constant Improvement

In the course of marriage, many women fail to improve themselves, and so they lose out when other better educated or enlightened women sway their husband's attention. This is not to encourage or excuse unfaithfulness in any man, but the bottom line is this: Do not allow yourself to be left behind as your husband improves himself and expands his horizon and worldview. It is possible for a wife to find out that she no longer fits into her husband's lifestyle or group of friends because she failed to be part of his agenda for development. Such a woman might be quick to narrate the story of how she "made" her husband by slaving to pay his school fees or by demonstrating self-denial in other ways. The sympathy of the world is with such women, but I am sure they need more than sympathy; they need their husbands! Every woman of God must avoid this pitfall, which many of their older sisters and mothers fell into with grave consequences. As our husbands improve, so must we. In fact, we must provoke improvement in our husbands so we can bring out the best in them.

Dear sister, God has work for us women to do, even when we are confronted with lack, fear, or failure, and we do well to concentrate as a matter of priority on this work. Sometimes we may experience fatigue after overcoming a major challenge that drained us emotionally or physically, but please press on.

Undoubtedly, the breakthroughs your marriage will witness will happen through collaborative efforts, and I dare say the same for the world. Families should collaborate and build stronger ties. Aside from making babies, some families hardly have any reason to collaborate; every effort should be made to improve on this. Please add the new word *collab* to your family dictionary/lexicon—as in, "Let's collab; let's do things together!"

Seven

The Power of Partnership

THE POWER OF partnership applies to all areas of life. As this book is primarily addressed to women who will contribute significantly to making their marriages succeed, I will discuss here the importance of partnership in a marriage. There is a common saying that "Behind every successful man is a woman." Over time, we heard another version that says, "*Beside* every successful man is a woman." Whichever version you subscribe to, the importance of a woman is being acknowledged, and that is good. There is also another common saying that "The man is the head of the family, while the woman is the neck." This saying goes to emphasize the influence of a woman in marriage. The Bible says, "Two are better than one" (Eccl. 4:9–11). It is important that the "two" should be in agreement in order to harness the power of partnership. The Bible also says, "One shall chase a thousand, and two shall chase ten thousand" (Deut. 32:30).

Women usually go into marriage with high ideals, hopes, and expectations but become frustrated over time when those expectations are not met and love and trust are broken. It is important to prepare women for marriage instead of leaving them to learn the pitfalls in relationships only by heartbreaking experiences. When a person loves another person, he or she becomes vulnerable to being hurt by that person. This is not a disincentive to love; it is a word of caution to prepare before falling in love and committing to marriage.

The only training or preparation some women get before they go into marriage are stories told from the grapevine, gossip on failed marriages, and television shows. They end up with only wrong or artificial information on marriage. Everyone works hard at maintaining this artificial life that they show the outside world—until reality hits like a thunderbolt. This has happened so often that there is now an unspoken expectation that every marriage will fail and that there are no good marriages anymore. Admittedly, this is due partly to societal pressures, but a marriage will perform better if both men and women are prepared for it before they go into it.

No woman should commit to a marriage until she has matured enough to handle responsibility and differences of opinion. You must prepare your heart and mind for marriage. We work hard at things we are committed to do, so make a definite commitment before marriage that you will make a success of it. There is no perfect marriage, since it is the union of two imperfect adults, yet there are good and happy marriages. No two marriages are alike, so every woman should desist from comparing her marriage with other marriages or being quick to judge some marriages as unhappy. Make your marriage what you want it to be by working on it with your husband. The next chapter deals with some factors that help promote good relationships.

Eight

_____

Factors that Promote
Good Relationships

Communication

COMMUNICATION IS VERY important in any
relationship and forms the bedrock of a successful
marriage. It is important to all the different issues
we will discuss throughout this book. The key to effective
communication is to connect—that is, to not be distant
from your partner. You must keep communication lines
open and accessible. Many women tend to have the
ability to remember vividly events that happened a long
time ago. In addition to this, they are able to string these
events together to make a strong point that will justify
their actions or reactions. Women also tend to go back
to unresolved grievances from decades ago. To resolve
conflicts, it is imperative to deal only with the issue at
hand and not bring up the past. Any other issues can be
discussed at a different time.

Do not bottle up your negative feelings and sit on
your hurt and anger. If you do, you will eventually

implode—turn your emotions inward and get sick—
or explode, and God help those around you! Just about
any little thing can trigger an explosion, so beware. It is
generally believed that women have many places to hide
things. Mary, the mother of Jesus, in Luke 2:19, was said
to have kept "all these things in her heart," constantly
dwelling on them. The difference, however, is that the
things Mary kept in her heart were positive things about
the prophecies concerning her son, Jesus. We can make
a decision about what to keep in our hearts and what we
want to dwell on. Let us dwell on positive things, as the
Apostle Paul admonished in Philippians 4:8:

> And now, brothers, as I close this letter,
> let me say this one more thing: fix your
> thoughts on what is true and good and right.
> Think about things that are pure and lovely,
> and dwell on the fine good things in others.
> Think about what you can praise God for
> and be glad about.

Another thing women must be aware of is differences
in opinions on important matters. Part of improving
communication is understanding the other person's point
of view in order to make intelligent decisions.

Also, every woman should learn to speak the truth in
love. Remember that "grace and truth came by Jesus Christ"
(John 1:17, KJV). We, too, need to speak the truth with
grace—that is, to always give loving, gracious acceptance.
Some of us are good at speaking the truth but are short on

love. If people feel safe to share their deep thoughts with us, we need to speak from a point of sensitivity and caring.

Failure of Communication

Sometimes we fail to communicate, even when we desperately want to. It is not only in marriage that communication fails, as the piece below, culled from *Daily Encounter* by Richard Innes, shows:

> Not so long ago, two of my sisters and a brother-in-law from Australia visited us here in California. John, my brother-in-law, came down with a heavy cold and was feeling lousy. He went to a local pharmacy to get some medication—or to try to get some. He spoke to the pharmacist (chemist, as he called him) and said in his heavy Aussie accent, "I have a dreadful cold and need some medicine todie."
>
> "I beg your pardon," replied the pharmacist. "You want what?"
>
> "I want some medicine todie."
>
> "I can't do that for you," the pharmacist declared.
>
> "But I'm feeling very sick and need help todie," John repeated, and for the life of him he couldn't understand why the pharmacist wouldn't help him. John ended up walking out of the pharmacy and came home very frustrated.
>
> John and the pharmacist were both

speaking the same language, but neither one understood the other. When John, with his heavy Australian accent, said, "I need help todie," in American, he was actually saying, "I need help today." Needless to say, when we translated for him, we all had a fit of laughter.[1]

In relationships, however, miscommunication can be the cause of considerable misunderstanding and conflict. Two partners or friends may be saying the same thing but each interprets it differently. We think that what we think is what the other was thinking when they didn't say what we thought they said and didn't know what they were thinking. That's how confusing miscommunication can be!

So, again, all of us (including myself) need to stick to the old remedy by counting to ten when we are upset by what another has said—before we fly off the handle. Before jumping to a wrong conclusion, ask, "I'm confused. Did I hear you correctly?" Explain what you heard, and then ask, "Is this what you meant? If not, will you please explain so I don't misunderstand you?" We have only communicated effectively when the listener interprets and understands what we have said as closely as possible to our intended meaning—something we all need to work on when communicating.

Effective Communication

At the center of effective relationships is effective communication, which is sharing not only what we think, but much more what we feel. Eighty percent of close relating is at the feeling level, so we need to learn how to share honestly what we are feeling without blaming the other person for these feelings. Good communication is the heart and soul of intimacy.

Faulty communication causes many problems, and this is especially true in the home. In fact, one of the first steps to improving family relationships is improving family communication. Since the family starts with the husband and wife, the job of laying the foundation for family members to talk meaningfully to one another every day, show an interest in one other, give constant understanding and approval, and share and accept each other's feelings lies with them. Each member also needs to be given a say in family matters, and through practical compromises we can smooth family life and individual living.

Even though communication goes two ways and involves going beyond a person's words to hear what they have not said—by considering tone of voice, facial expressions, body language, and so on—it is important for all family members to say what they mean and not leave others to guess. The guessing game leads to misunderstanding and stress. So much of the joy of relationships will be lost if we always have to guess what the other person means.

Dealing With Conflict

Wherever people live together, some form of conflict is inevitable. Differences and frustrations (including money, work, relatives and sexual problems) need to be talked about and resolved. If they aren't, the effects of that eventually manifests through depression, ill health, or broken relationships.

Many reactions to conflict, however, are overreactions caused by unresolved conflicts from the past. This is worth repeating: resolve past issues. We may be able to hide our problems before we are married, but once the knot is tied, those problems surface sooner or later. For example, a person who has a poor relationship with one or both parents will not be prepared for a healthy relationship with their spouse's parents unless they work on their issues. Since many of us grow up in families that have their own issues, this is a weakness we must overcome prayerfully and consciously.

When we overreact, we need to find the underlying problem, accept responsibility for it, deal with it, and not blame others. Otherwise conflicts will remain unresolved. Unresolved problems over time will lead to hostility, the eventual breakdown of communication, and estrangement between couples. Taking responsibility by admitting when we overreact is being mature. Try to verbalize your feelings without blaming the other person for them. If overreaction is a habit of yours, do not hesitate to seek help from a competent pastor or counselor. Admitting when we need help is a sign of maturity.

Also, couples will do well to avoid inflammatory words like, "You never," "You always," or, "That was how you said it last time when…" Such statements are generalizations and rarely true. Cutting people down to size, dishing out put-downs, and deriding others also need to be avoided. These are veiled expressions of hostility that provoke retaliation. It is much kinder to admit when you are feeling hurt or angry.

Many studies have compared happily married couples

with unhappily married ones. Happily married couples are more likely to talk to each other and have a wider range of subjects to talk about. They also convey the feeling that they are interested in and understand what was is being said to them. They show more sensitivity to each other's feelings. Their nonverbal cues are well understood between them. Most importantly, they preserve the communication channels and keep them open no matter what happens.

Enrich Your Lives Together

If you are committed to someone, you want to make them happy. If you are committed to a cause, you do all you can to propagate and defend it. Spending more time together is equally important for strengthening family relationships. When couples are too busy for this, they definitely have a problem! Families need to spend more time together and participate in activities that encourage togetherness.

When they arise, conflicts need to be faced and handled effectively. The reality is that there are no innocent parties in any marriage conflict. Each person contributes something. Only as each person admits, owns up, and takes responsibility for his or her reactions, and especially overreactions, can a healthy relationship be sustained. "When a married couple says they've never had a disagreement, they are lying, have poor memory, or one partner has been made a zero in the relationship," says Clark Hensley, director of the Mississippi Christian Action Commission.

Give Up the Right to Always Be Right

It is a mark of immaturity to always want to be right. It also shows a person to be insecure. We are not only to speak the truth in love, but also to grow up and mature in all areas of our lives. Part of growing up includes humility and respect for others and their viewpoints.

Speak Softly

Most of us tend to raise our voices when we are angry. One effective way to calm people who yell when they speak is to speak softly. Yelling begets yelling! As Michel de Montaigne said, "He who establishes his argument by noise and command shows that his reason is weak." The Bible says in Proverbs 15:1, "A soft answer turns away wrath, but grievous words stir up hostility."

Also, pray about yourself. You may benefit by knowing what you are contributing to a conflict when you pray sincerely.

Forgiveness

Forgiveness is another essential factor for healthy relationships. Many marriages are gradually eroded and eventually destroyed because one person is unable to forgive. You need to forgive as well as receive forgiveness from your husband. Do not give the impression that he is the recalcitrant person and the only one always in need of forgiveness. A woman who continually brings up things her husband did or said in the past continues to weaken the bond between them and erects a wall of coldness that will lead to hostility. A woman must not be hostile towards her husband, even when there is a problem at hand. As God forgives us when we confess our wrongs, we also need to forgive each other. Colossians 3:13 says, "Be gentle and ready to forgive; never hold grudges. Remember, the Lord forgave you, so you must forgive others." *Forgive and let go of grudges.* When couples lash out and hurt each other or withdraw when they feel hurt or angry, a wall of resentment and suspicion builds up between them, and this blocks out love and makes closeness impossible. As the Bible teaches, "Don't let the sun go down with you still angry; get over it quickly" (Eph. 4:26). All negative feelings need to be resolved as quickly as possible so forgiveness can be sought and given and closeness maintained.

Clear communication, cooperation, handling conflicts creatively, and forgiveness are all vital for family harmony. However, the most important need is to put God at the center of your home. He can do a much better job of keeping your family than you can if you will daily commit your life to him and follow His divine order for the home.

Build a Healthy Marriage

Going by outward appearances, some husbands and wives look like the perfect couple. They are seen everywhere together and dress alike when they attend events, and people around them say, "Theirs is a match made in heaven. If any couple would make it, they would." Then, five years and three children later, to everyone's shock, their marriage ends in divorce. The causes of broken marriages are often complex and numerous and may be difficult to cover completely in a book, but we can work to prevent heartache and divorce in our marriages, and this is the sole aim of this book.

Growing Together in Love

Physical attraction can be very exhilarating and can lead to love, but, in itself, it is not love and may simmer over time. We call physical attraction "falling in love." The trouble with this kind of love is that it is just as easy to fall out of it. It's sad that as exciting as physical attraction is—and while it may be a good beginning for a relationship—it is not enough to keep a relationship growing and enduring. But we can hold on to some of its allure in marriage by keeping the romance alive. It is even said that keeping romance alive is as important as is keeping true love alive. This does not happen by chance, though; it takes considerable effort and needs to be made a high priority in a marriage. The marriages that succeed have other ingredients of success, and we discuss some of them in various parts of this book.

Work at the growth and health of your marriage through effective communication, giving your marriage priority over other relationships, commitment that flows out of love and, of course, forgiveness.

Grow in Maturity

Selfishness, blaming others for our problems, overreacting, being oversensitive, having our feelings hurt too easily, insecurity, lack of healthy boundaries, defensiveness, expecting perfection from oneself and other—all of these are symptoms of immaturity, and they destroy meaningful relationships. It bears repeating that to have a healthy marriage we need to take responsibility for resolving all of our personal problems and grow into maturity.

Build Commitment

Among other things, love is a commitment from one imperfect person to another. Everybody has their faults; but as each partner admits his or hers, shows commitment to overcoming them, and accepts his or her partner with their faults, a healthy and strong relationship can be built.

Have Realistic Expectations

There is a story of a woman who has been divorced twice and says that she just cannot find a man to measure up to her father. The world of make believe—Nollywood, Bollywood, Hollywood, and the other "woods"—has fueled a lot of unrealistic expectations, especially among women. The glamour magazines that display women (and sometimes men) with unblemished skin and perfect bodies can seriously distort our views of beauty, sex, and love and leave us with totally unrealistic expectations. To make matters worse, most of these unrealistic expectations are unwritten and unarticulated! They just nibble at our subconscious minds without our notice and wreak havoc there. To have genuine marriages, we need to get real and down to earth! It may be helpful to say what our expectations are so we know what we are up against. We can also review them as we come face to face with them.

Have Similar Interests and Purposes

Over the years, if one partner goes in one direction and the other in a totally different one, little by little they will drift apart. A couple does not need to share *all* their interests, but it is important that they develop enough common ones that they can enjoy them together. Pulling in one direction can grow a marriage and help a couple set targets and goals and achieve them. Not having shared interests is like being in a tug-of-war, with husband and wife pulling in different directions. This way you will only scatter and destroy, not build; and the success of your marriage is based on what you can build together, not what you can destroy. We can link this need to have similar interests with the need to develop ourselves as our husbands climb the ladder of success in their endeavors.

Develop a Strong Spiritual Commitment

Research has shown that the spiritual commitment of each partner has a positive effect on their marriage. We are much more than intellectual and physical beings. We are also spiritual beings, with an innate urge to relate with God. Committing your lives to God as a couple and trusting Him to guide you makes a solid foundation for any relationship. This will create a much greater chance of not only making it together, but of also having a very happy marriage relationship.

Unintelligent Communication

By unintelligent communication, I mean communication in which the law of passing information from one person to another in a way that it is understood is broken. A Christian couple tried out this unintelligent communication method when they decided to keep malice. The wife decided to write her husband to say that there was no cooking gas, so their children would have no food to eat the following morning. She put it where she thought her husband would see it so he could buy the gas, but he did not read the note. You guessed what happened: There was no gas to cook for the family, particularly their very young children, the following morning. I used to hear variants of this story, but I found it hard to believe they were real life issues! I thought we as Christians have become wiser and now know better than to behave this way. Please keep talking with your spouse no matter how serious the situation is, and learn to forgive each other. Another wise thing to learn is that no matter how grave a situation is, you will only resolve it by talking. Problems are not resolved by refusing to talk to each other.

THOUGHT AND PRAYER

I gain better insight by trying to understand what the other person is saying. I am also more relaxed and less antagonistic when I do not impute a wrong motive to what is being said before I have processed it in my mind.

Dear God, please help me to listen to my husband both with my ears and my heart and bring out the best in him in my interactions. In Jesus' name, amen.

Different Ways to Apologize

Does your husband apologize when he offends you? It may be helpful to learn that you can know when your husband is trying to apologize without actually saying, "I'm sorry"! Take the cues and enjoy yourself while your husband is trying to unlearn the bad habit of not saying sorry. I learned this from an older friend even before I got married. According to her, each time her husband offended her, he had this habit of saying, "Ruth, it's been so long since we went out together. Let's go out this evening." As you would expect, she would say no because she was still offended. After a while, she got to understand that this was her husband's way of apologizing. She began to take advantage of his offers! I call her a wise woman indeed.

Find out your husband's special, innovative way(s) of apologizing, and dig in and enjoy every bit of it! Do not take yourself too seriously by brooding over human foibles, since you have your flaws also. It may be challenging when your spouse offends you repeatedly, yet it is possible to discuss and help each other get over bad habits. Do not always pass the blame to your spouse when you have misunderstandings. Think through the issues and be willing to make necessary adjustments when it is pragmatic to do so.

Nine

Love

LOVE AND RESPECT are important ingredients for any good relationship, including marriage, but they cannot be made to happen by a fiat or by order. Charles Finney says, "Love is bringing about the highest good in the life of another individual."

> "Love is bringing about the highest good in the life of another individual."
> —Charles Finney

Falling in love can be the start of a loving relationship, but lasting relationships don't just happen; they are nurtured. In many ways, nurturing a relationship is like tending a garden. If it is neglected, it dies. It needs constant care and cultivation. I guess we all know by now that love is more than a feeling; it is an action, and it can influence everything we do if we are thoughtful.

Every woman must love her husband, and no woman should marry a man

We must commit to doing good to our husbands all the days of our lives. This is a vow every woman who marries a man must make before God.

she does not love. Whichever way love develops between a couple, it has to be nurtured to the point where it becomes a way of life for them, and I suggest the woman show the way. It is interesting how the things we give return to us. Instead of going out in search of friends, let each of us cultivate the habit of being a friend.

> When we consider the blessings of God—the gifts that add beauty and joy to our lives, that enable us to keep going through stretches of boredom and even suffering—friendship is very near the top.
> —Donald W. McCullough, *Mastering Personal Growth*[1]

It is in the interest of every woman to plant it in her husband's heart that she loves him. This must be done before marriage and must become deeply ingrained in his heart over the years. We must verbalize and demonstrate it until it takes root in our minds and in our husbands' minds. We must commit to doing good to our husbands all the days of our lives. This is a vow every woman who marries a man must make before God.

Proverbs 31:11–12 says something similar: "Her husband can trust her and she will richly satisfy his needs. She will not hinder him, but help him all her life." In a world full of wickedness and uncertainty, this is a serious task, but the good news is that God has not stopped helping those who trust Him. While most women profess love for their husbands, many fail to demonstrate it when they are offended or when their needs are not met. They are quick to remind the man that they are responsible for his success or say any hurtful thing that might come to their hearts at the time.

Love Is More Than Sex

I agree with Richard Innes in his writing, "The Art of Staying in Love," where he said:

> *Love is more than sex.* Love is much more than a physical relationship. It is also an emotional relationship. The man who ignores the emotional needs of his wife and expects to receive a warm response in bed is inviting frustration. Women are not machines to be turned on at will. Sex starts in the kitchen at six, not in the bedroom at nine. A long-lasting physical relationship is the result of an ongoing healthy emotional relationship.
>
> On the other hand, the wife who no longer shows any interest in her husband's life outside the home feels totally shocked when she discovers that one of the younger

women at the office has. Many men (and women too) who get involved in extra-marital activity, don't do it so much for sexual reasons but for companionship—someone who will listen to them and make them feel important and appreciated.

Love is romance. I read about one woman who had been married for twenty-five years. She was in her front yard when the newlywed man from across the street arrived home from work. His wife rushed out the door to greet him and they stood embracing for a long time.

The observer got the message. When her husband came home that evening she did likewise. The rewards of all such romantic gestures are well worth the effort. And men, don't forget that our ladies love a rose from time to time and other "little things" that make them feel loved and important. A good tip for keeping romance alive, as one person suggested, is to have an affair—with your wife?[2]

Love Is Spiritual

We often focus on the feelings (emotional) and physical parts of love, sometimes limiting it to how we feel towards our husbands, physical touch, and love making. We however know that feelings may change so our love needs an anchor—a safety net—to secure it. The greatest love story ever told is still the love God demonstrated toward us by sending Jesus Christ to pay the price for our sins. What better way to secure our love relationships than in God? I am inclined to believe that most people claim to love God and making Him the source and stay in our relationships can be a stabilizing factor in marriage.

The Bible in 1 John 4:8 says God is love; this buttresses the fact that marriage based on love is spiritual. Love is undergirded by the Word of God and in marriage it goes beyond physical and emotional dimensions of living even though these are very important. It is important to make this spiritual connection so that women (and men of course) who go into marriage will begin to see the God connection in their relationships. This will enhance relationships as we become acutely aware of God's stake in our marriages. This will enhance commitment and respect in the marriage. As we open our hearts to the love of God, we are better able to love our husbands and other family members.

Most of us know from personal experience that our spiritual lives can help to greatly enrich our love lives. Improving your spiritual life is well worth a try, if you have not done it already. It would be wise to not wait until you experience problems in your marriage before trying this out.

Presence

Being present with your spouse is not only being with him physically; it also means giving him your undivided attention. It includes being sensitive to his feelings and aware of his needs. It means not only hearing with your ears but, much more so, with your heart. In the busy world we live in now, it takes special effort to assure your

A sense of
responsibility
is the clearest
indication of
maturity.
—John Maxwell

husband of your presence and to be there for him.

Accepting Responsibility

> A sense of responsibility is the clearest indication of maturity.
>
> —JOHN MAXWELL[4]

If we desire to stay in love, it is imperative that each of us accepts responsibility y for resolving our inner conflicts that cause dissension in our present relationships. Most of us bring the excess baggage of unresolved issues from the past into our present relationships. For example, in the study of behavior, there is a phenomenon called "transferred aggression." It manifests when a person transfers his or her frustration and anger with one person onto another person, who may be totally unaware of and not responsible for the hostility. We could not have been responsible f or our upbringing, but we are totally responsible for what we do about resolving any negative effects our past had on us. We are also responsible for conducting ourselves properly in the way we relate with our husbands. We cannot make a habit of apologizing for saying the wrong things because we were angry or frustrated over an issue.

Be Sincere With Yourself

There is an old story about a time when the viceroy of Naples was visiting Spain. He visited the harbor and saw a galley ship of convicts used to pull the oars. The viceroy went aboard and asked the men why they were there. One man said that the judge was bribed to convict him. Another said that his enemies paid people to bear false witness against him. Still another said his best friend had lied to protect himself. Finally, one man said, "I'm here because I deserve to be. I wanted money and I stole a purse." With this, the viceroy said to the captain, "Here are all these innocent men and only one wicked man in their midst. Let us release this man lest he infect the others." The man was set free and pardoned.

The moral is: Instead of blaming everyone but yourself, accept responsibility when you have done wrong.

Commitment

> True love is a commitment of one imperfect person to another.
>
> —ANONYMOUS

True love is a commitment of one imperfect person to another.
—Anonymous

Commitment flows out of love. It is difficult to show commitment to someone you do not love. Love should breed commitment over time. The rough patches in marriage are better handled when there is commitment. It is commitment that will make a woman take care of her husband in bad as well as good times. Commitment to your husband will breed commitment to the family. Marriage is a demonstration of love that requires a lot of sacrifice and lasts as long as we live! This kind of commitment means that one person will not try to manipulate the other to get his or her own way, but will at all times maintain open and honest communication. This isn't easy, but it is the way of love.

As this book is a practical manual for the woman who wants to love her husband forever, I will share a real-life example of commitment to a man and a family.

Mrs. Oyeyemi Ajayi is a woman of God and the wife of my elder brother, Mr. Oladejo Ajayi. This couple never ceases to amaze me with their love and devotion to one another. In the Christian assembly in Lagos where they fellowship, they are highly respected because their commitment to one another is clear. Mrs. Ajayi is so committed to her family that every day, she finds out where each person is, keeps appointments on behalf of each member, and meets needs for prayers, counseling, and coordination. Her husband fondly refers to her as his managing director because he travels often on international consultancy trips. In addition to her daily tasks, she keeps in constant touch with their children, both in Nigeria and abroad. She ensures there is contact among members of the family, and she is a woman of incredible faith and energy. She has become the matriarch and an invaluable asset even to the larger family. Her presence of mind and attention to detail is exemplary. Even when she is displeased, she handles it so effortlessly, never allowing anger or resentment to cloud her judgment. Her comportment is outstanding! She is indeed a virtuous woman worthy of emulation.

I recommend that every married woman show this level of love and commitment to the cause of her family and to God. We have to wholeheartedly work on being more committed to our husbands, children, and families. Commitment to our families is a key way through which we demonstrate love for God, because the health of the family is at the heart of His plan for mankind.

You Are a Private Garden

Every married woman is a private garden and should see herself as such. No trespassing is allowed.

> My darling bride is like a private garden, a spring that no one else can have, a fountain of my own.
>
> You are like a lovely orchard bearing precious fruit, with the rarest of perfumes; nard and saffron, calamus and cinnamon, and perfume from every other incense tree, as well as myrrh and aloes and every other lovely spice.
>
> You are a garden fountain, a well of living water, refreshing as the stream from Lebanon mountains.

> Come north wind, awaken; come south
> wind, blow upon my garden and waft its
> lovely perfume to my beloved. Let him
> come into his garden and eat its choicest
> fruits.
>
> —Song of Solomon 4:12–16

Even as I write this, I applaud all women; we are simply an incredible treasure! If ever a woman considered cheating on her husband, this should help her perish the thought. It's so beautiful. If you do not really feel treasured, start working on the factors causing this. Some of us women are just not aware of who we are and what we have been endowed with. This should help give you another perspective

Maintaining the Dignity of Man

In relating with every person, there is a certain God-given dignity that we must not treat lightly. This dignity has nothing to do with your perception of the person and should not be violated by trying to shame or scorn them. This is something we should all bear in mind in dealing with others.

Submission in Marriage

Ephesians 5:22-24 says:

> You wives must submit to your husband's
> leadership in the same way you submit to
> the Lord.
>
> For a husband is in charge of his wife

in the same way Christ is in charge of his body the Church. He gave his very life to take care of it and be its Saviour.

So you wives must willingly obey your husbands in everything, just as the Church obeys Christ.

The word *submit* means to yield to authority or be accountable to somebody. The Life Application Bible (NLT) has this comment on Ephesians 5:22–24:

> Submitting to another person is an often misunderstood concept. It does not mean becoming a doormat. Christ—at whose name "every knee must bow, in heaven and on earth and under the earth" (Philippians 2:10)—submitted his will to the Father, and we honour Christ by following his example...In a marriage relationship, both husband and wife are called to submit. For the wife, this means willingly following her husband's leadership in Christ. For the husband it means putting aside his own interests in order to care for his wife.

A wife will have little problem submitting to her husband's leadership if she is convinced that he has her interest at heart. Every family needs to revisit the issue of submission in order to improve their relationships.

Respect

It is important for a woman to respect her husband, whatever station he finds himself in life. If you cannot respect a man, please do not marry him! Some women think they can only respect their husbands when he is rich or strong or articulate. The Christian woman, and indeed all women, must respect their husbands if they will get the best out of their partnership and make a success of their family life. When we respect our husbands, we teach those around us to respect him as well, and our daughters to do same to their husbands when they get married. We should not scream at our husbands or shout them down when they want to speak.

Also, calling your husband by his first name may not be a sign of disrespect, but it is advisable that this be discussed and an agreement reached on it. Do not insist on calling your husband by his first name if he does not like it. Life is better when we take the other person's feelings into consideration. There are so many endearing names we can call our husbands if they prefer not to be called by their first name. And please, do not give your husband that "how dare you" glare or "bad eye" when he wants to talk to you, even if he has offended you.

As Africans, we show respect by the way we speak to people, and this should be observed in the family. Respect is important for the emotional well-being of the man, so every woman must respect her husband even when she disagrees with him. Women generally tend to be more vocal than men, so you must guard against shouting your husband down or deriding him when you have disagreements. Each person should be free to present a point of view without being shouted down or insulted. Bear in mind that it is always better to discuss than to argue. Anger should not be cited as an excuse for rudeness and bad behavior. Rudeness shows poor breeding and lack of class and should not be seen among Christian women. All sharp tongues should be tamed by prayers and counseling.

Feeding Your Husband

Providing meals in the home is a primary responsibility of the woman, with help from her husband. It is still said that the way to a man's heart is through his stomach. A woman needs to hold the reins of her husband's heart by every means possible. Taking care of feeding in the home can present a challenge in our modern society, where both men and women have jobs that require their attention through the day, five or six days a week. In view of this, it is preferred that husbands help their wives with some of the chores in the home. However, if your husband is averse to assisting, do not make this a sore point in your marriage. Remember, sometimes it takes time and effort to change learned habits. This is where planning together as a family will help to sort out the issues. Prayerfully seek the services and assistance of other helpful resources. These social paid services are resources available to all working-class women who are willing to use them cautiously.

Knowledge has increased tremendously, and so have the options for keeping healthy. It is important to ensure that your husband and children eat balanced and healthy foods. The effect of food on the health and vitality of a man should be kept in mind. It is better to adopt a healthy lifestyle than to seek treatment for diet-related health problems. Myles Munroe once said, "You must watch what you eat; you cannot have a big dream and a poor diet." It takes a deliberate effort to establish a routine for a healthy diet, but the gains will prove well worth it over a lifetime and will be a legacy to your children. A woman has to learn the timeless principle of balancing strength with grace in order to get the best for her husband and children.

Part Three

Ten

___

Some Practical Suggestions

Master of Cues

THIS CHAPTER IS for women only. Men must obtain the consent of their wives before reading this!)

Just as a woman is able to pick up on cues, she must also be able to drop them. Cues are unspoken suggestions on a preferred way of doing things. Cues are good catalysts for enhanced romance in a marriage and could be looks, gestures, or body language.

As a woman, you are endowed to take charge of your turf and determine what goes on there. Used for good, cues can tremendously improve marriage and family life, bringing out the best in everyone in an atmosphere of love and trust—and with the added advantage of fun.

When a young Christian female is being brought up, she is taught to be chaste and modest; then she gets married and everyone expects her to metamorphose overnight into an alluring, delectable wife. These two roles are far apart; therefore, we need to bridge the gap and teach the Christian female how to ease into her role as a spouse. Pre-marital counseling and preparation is needed for both males and females.

Thankfully, God created humans with the natural instincts they need to relate sexually—which is frowned upon before marriage—without necessarily having to be taught; and when in love, these instincts are activated. Give your husband an alluring look—a look that screams, "I am available!" I am sure you can do that with the pounding going on in your heart as you look at your husband.

The next suggestion will be even easier—body language. We use body language in many different ways, including the pursuit of love. You will have to experiment and come up with your unique language for your love nest. Give your husband some private, intimate ultimatums from time to time. It must be something positive, exhilarating and value-adding to your relationship.

A woman has the capacity to transform any good thing in her family into a legacy for the next generation by working consistently and persistently on it. Please look out for these good things which you will, with God's help, transform into a legacy for future generations.

Dress to Please

The modern girl dresses to please herself, but she has another person to consider when she dresses. Make yourself desirable; dress to please your husband. There are ways to convince your husband that he is important to you, and taking him into consideration as you plan your wardrobe is one. I believe your husband wants to please

God, so if you dress to please him, you will still be on course! Perhaps some of those items your husband would love are for an audience of one—him alone. There will be no one else to see you, so go on! You need to capture your husband's attention totally so that others outside who might be looking to do the same will be beaten at their game. The weapons of our warfare in this matter are both spiritual and physical; use both!

Ownership of Property

At the risk of being branded an extinct species, I believe married couples should own property together. The documentation on the properties should indicate joint ownership. Where one partner builds a house in his or her name, it should not be treated as a secret. Some women build houses without the knowledge of their husbands. This should be condemned because it undermines the unity of the family. This practice of separate ownership of property was very common among the older generation, especially in polygamous families. In Christ, polygamy is forbidden, so there is no excuse for such behavior. Every couple should make investments together for the future and ensure provision for their children. Each time a woman makes a major purchase or investment without informing her husband, she weakens their bond and sabotages her own home. It is like working against the interests of the family to whom she is giving so much of her time and affection, and it shows a lack of trust or commitment or some underlying problems. If a condition exists that makes joint ownership of property impractical, the couple should seek counsel to address it and to restore stability to their marriage.

Joint Financial Accounts

By a joint account, I mean one account that is operated by the husband and the wife. Having a joint account has its advantages and disadvantages. The advantage is that the husband and wife know the amount of money that is available to them, making for transparency and accountability in their expenditures. If a couple finds this agreeable, both of them should be co-signatories to the account, so that no spouse can withdraw money without the knowledge of the other. Everything must be done in love and with due consideration for the other partner.

The disadvantage of having a joint account is that spending patterns differ between spouses, and this could lead to disagreements. My husband and I do not have a joint account, but we believe in joint responsibility so that family needs are met. For those of us who give most of our earnings to worthy causes, a joint account may be a nightmare for our partners if they do not share or cannot match our propensity to give.

In the course of writing this book, my church, New Estate Baptist Church, Abuja, organized a family enrichment program that proved a very good opportunity to enrich this book with more real-life examples. I have seized this opportunity with both hands and with gratitude to God and the many couples who made their life experiences available to me.

Let me introduce engineer Clement Oke and his soulmate, Dr. Yetunde Oke. This lovely couple has been married for thirty-two years and have kept a joint account all this time. They recommend a joint account for couples based on their experience, and I have included their contribution:

> We opened a joint account before marriage with a mandate of either of us to withdraw money in order to plan for the wedding, having jointly decided that our parents should contribute minimally to activities other than feeding people at the wedding. The joint account practice continued on to ownership of foreign accounts after marriage to ensure transparency within the family. This also caters for a situation of permanent loss in case of demise of either of us. Ultimately, the concept of a joint account was extended to a family account in Nigeria. A major advantage of this is the avoidance of transfer of assets in case of death of either spouse. In addition, both parties do also have the liberty of operating individual accounts.[1]

With an example as beautiful as this, it is clear there is something to be said for joint accounts between Christian couples. I wish to draw attention to the similarity in the background of this wonderful couple and, above all, the genuineness of their Christian faith and love for each other. I believe this has helped them operate a joint account successfully.

Handling Money Matters

Money matters usually prove tricky, and it may be wise to consult professionals when dealing with them. Whether a couple keeps a joint account or not, someone still has to take the lead in money matters, including decisions on spending, major investments, and disbursement. These decisions should be jointly taken, with the husband overseeing them if he has better financial knowledge than his wife. If, however, the wife has a better grasp of financial issues, she should work in the interest of the family with the full support of her husband.

John Gardner said, on philosophers and plumbers:

> An excellent plumber is infinitely more admirable than an incompetent philosopher. A society which scorns excellence in plumbing because it is a humble activity and tolerates shoddiness in philosophy because it is an exalted activity will have neither good plumbing nor good philosophy. Neither its pipes nor its theories will hold water.[2]

I agree. We are not talking about plumbing here, but Gardner's statement can be related to managing finances in the family. If we want to have a good financial blueprint and money management in the interest of the family, whoever can make this happen should be in charge of the family's money. The spouse who earns more should not automatically be the one to make the decisions on money.

Most of the issues that snowball into conflicts can be

discussed ahead of time to prevent this. Prevention, they say, is always better than a cure. As couples look forward to building winning teams, decisions become easier to make because there are no hidden agendas and the decisions are in the interests of the family. We have to work relentlessly at reaching this point of full disclosure in order to harness its gains.

Sexual Relationship

Men and women see the need for sex differently. To a woman, sex flows out of affection, while it is a deeper need for a man. A woman wants to sort out her differences with her husband before having sex, but a man may be more receptive to his wife's ideas if they are presented after sex. I believe women need more counseling on how men and women see sex.

The Bible says about conjugal rights: "For a girl who marries no longer has full rights to her own body, for her husband then has his rights to it too; and in the same way the husband no longer has full rights to his own body, for it belongs also to his wife" (1 Cor. 7:4). Marriage is honorable and must remain so as we commit to our marriage vows and partners. Sex should not be used a bargaining tool for extorting things from our husbands or for showing that we are aggrieved. Discussion is a better and more effective tool in resolving our differences in marriage.

Sex is one of the strongest motivators on earth and can be used positively or negatively. The advertising industry has and continues to exploit it. Sex, or the thought of it, is used to advertise just about any product you can think of.

Sex is ordained by God for married people and

should not be allowed to become a tool of oppression or suppression by either partner. It is also not a game that can be played with any partner in sight, no matter the level of physical attraction. Sex is not like hunger for food, which can be satisfied without much thought; sexual appetite must be satisfied within the confines of marriage. In line with this, every woman who plans to get married must be ready to commit to the sanctity of marriage.

Supporting Love

Love is the number one reason people give for getting married, yet lack of love is the reason for most divorces. How did love take flight from the interval between marriage and divorce? It just goes to show that love can grow when nurtured or die when taken for granted. Believe me, romantic love is exhilarating; you need to enjoy it to know its allure! It is like what sailors call the "call of the sea," which only they can know.

We must find a way to hold on to some of its allure in the years after marriage. It's all too easy to settle into a routine after marriage, especially when the children begin to show up. A woman must fan the embers of love in her marriage in creative ways. Granted, it is easy to be engaged in romance when there are no outstanding bills to be paid and everything in life is going according to plan, but challenges should not sound the death knell of romance in marriage. The things couples do together to keep romance in their marriages do not have to be expensive to be exciting. Put on your thinking caps, ladies! Some women are upwardly mobile and high fliers at work, but where their marriages are concerned they demonstrate an abysmal level of incompetence. Could it be that we have to change a mindset or just think through these things?

At Home and at Work

It is my heart's desire to see a new crop of married divas doing well at home and at work, and I need your cooperation and commitment on this. Believe me, not all men are bad and unreliable; you can make your husband and sons part of the pool of these good and reliable men that will commit to God's purpose for themselves and the world. People like to work for their own interests, and the best way to get a person committed to an idea is to show him how it benefits him. This is described as social inclusion, and it can be applied in almost all spheres of human endeavor. If we work steadily in an inclusive manner, our husbands will come to the reality that if we do well, it will favor them and our children. When a husband believes his wife's success is his success, he will become a partner in working towards it.

Career women, it's time to change this perception we create that our work is more important than our marriage because it gives us economic power and financial freedom. Our careers or professions allow us to contribute more effectively to the success of our families; they are not in conflict or competition with our families. Your husband would not be made to believe he is in direct competition with your career or work if you apply wisdom in this area.

Eleven

This Man Can't Go It Alone!

It is only a
woman that
can make a
man become
the parody of
himself.
—French
proverb

D EAR READER, HAVE you noticed that your husband can't go it alone and that in spite of what is said or unsaid, he needs your support? Have you also noticed that a mature man who is unmarried, no matter how wealthy or highly placed, is regarded as unserious or sometimes even irresponsible? There is a need in the life of a man that only a woman can meet, and that is a privilege given to us as women. A good woman builds her home while a bad one scatters it. Proverbs 12:1 says, "A wise woman builds her house, while a foolish woman tears hers down by her own efforts." "It is only a woman that can make a man become the parody of himself" (French proverb[1]).

Develop a Sense of Self-Worth

"A wise woman builds her house, while a foolish woman tears hers down by her own efforts."
— Proverbs 12:1

I once heard that we are as sick as the people we are attracted to. To those of us who relate with God through the finished work of Jesus Christ on the cross, we know that healing is available to us in all areas of our lives. Each of us can access this healing for ourselves, our spouses or partners, and our family. Some women are difficult to love because they are tied up in knots—full of contradictions, unresolved issues, and turmoil in their hearts. Let me quickly say that they can access healing through a relationship with Jesus Christ. There is also the need to resolve some of these issues through Christian counseling and, where needed, deliverance should be administered to them by their pastors or other mature Christians. These women need help in order to be who God created them to be. A woman must bring a sense of self-worth into a relationship before that relationship can become worthwhile to her, her spouse or partner, and family.

Develop a robust sense of self-worth. Be natural; remember, you are a nurturer and giver. It does not matter what your family background is. Of course, a good family background is always preferable, but you can make something good of your life starting from where you are right now.

Richard Innes tells this story, entitled "Blame Game or Wise Choice," in *Daily Encounter*:

> Two young boys were raised in the home of an alcoholic father. As young men, they each went their own way. Years later, a psychologist who was analyzing what drunkenness does to children in the home searched out these two men. One had turned out to be like his father, a hopeless alcoholic. The other had turned out to be a teetotaler.
>
> The counselor asked the first man, "Why did you become an alcoholic?" He asked the second, "Why did you become a teetotaler?" They both gave an identical answer in these words: "What else could you expect when you had a father like mine?"[2]

It's not what happens to us in life but how we react to it that makes the difference. Every human being in the same situation has the possibilities of choosing how he will react, either positively or negatively.

Elfrieda Nikkel, in her article, "Did You Know You Are Someone Special?" tells the story of a girl named Marjorie who grew up with a sense of worthlessness.

Again and again, her father said she would never accomplish anything in life. He told her she was a loser and that anything she did try was sure to end in failure.

With these words ringing in her ears, Marjorie grew up looking for someone who would love her and see her as a person of worth. This led her into relationships that were disappointing to her, ending in pain and devastation with yet more proof that she was worthless and unlovable.[3]

Maybe you can identify with Marjorie and your story is much like hers. Nikkel ends the article with a question: Where does our sense of self-worth come from?

It is true that the foundation for a person's self-worth is laid in the home. Words that we hear in our home can build or tear down our worth as a person. The Bible speaks of words of life and death in Proverbs 18:21, where it says, "Death and life are in the power of the tongue." As we hear words of affirmation and encouragement, they are words of life to us, while words of criticism and belittlement are words of death. Other people, like teachers, friends, employers, and spouses, add to the collection of life-giving or death words in a person's heart. Over time, a person begins to see themselves in the light of these words.

If we look in the Scriptures, we see that God never meant it to be this way. He speaks words of life into the heart of every person. We read in Genesis that when God completed the creation of the world, He made man in His likeness or image. This likeness gave man—and later the woman He made, too—the capacity to think, to make decisions, to know right from wrong, to be creative, and to have the ability to communicate and have a personal relationship. Not only did God put this potential in the heart of man and woman, but He also gave them an assignment to use these abilities. They were told to rule over the things He had created and give to each a name.

Herein lies the potential to organize, care, and be in charge.

But the greatest evidence of our worth is that God loved us so much that He sent His Son to die for us when we were sinners and totally unlovable. We were worth it to Him. I totally agree with Elfrieda's parting shot: "You are special to God, and He wants to use you to speak 'words of life' into the lives of those around you."[4]

Don't beat yourself up over past mistakes and wrong motives. Your past cannot be anything else; you cannot change it, so learn from it. Identify what is in your power to change through hard work, attention to detail, and consistent practice, and focus on changing them. Turn those things you cannot change over to the Lord and move on with your life. Women are incredibly endowed to navigate the mountains and valleys of life; we just need to identify the issues and apply wisdom to them, with God's help.

Another thing to do is to remind yourself that the best in your life is not behind you, so stop behaving like Lot's wife. Remember her from Genesis 19? She looked back and permanently lost out on life.

I will admit that life's problems have the potential to disappoint, humiliate, and cause us all to stagnate, but we can rob them of power as we forge ahead, come what may, and in the process make the world a better place than we met it. Don't forget: Father Abraham, too, had problems before he became the man of faith we now sing about!

When we face difficult problems, we can choose to break them or be broken by them. We can become better or bitter; it's a matter of choice. King David in Psalm 139:14, said, "I am fearfully and wonderfully made." This should be the mantra of every woman of God since our robust sense of self-worth must be anchored on God's Word. I say this because any other way of developing self-worth puts us at risk of becoming conceited and haughty. These are traits that must not be seen in Christians, and definitely not in women who are the vessel through whom God will achieve His purpose for the world. God is not on the side of the proud; He resists them (James 4:6)! No woman wants to have God as an opponent, since we cannot achieve what we set out to achieve without His help.

I read an article on mental health by Gloria Ogunbadejo long ago in the *Sunday Punch* newspaper. It was about self-worth. Paraphrased, she said some females who dress immodestly, exposing private parts of their bodies, are probably plagued by low self-esteem. I found it intriguing to have a professional's opinion on what many consider merely a fashion issue.

Although there are many ways people may demonstrate immaturity and low self-esteem, it is important to find a solution to it because it affects our attitudes and all major relationships. If necessary, it would be good to seek professional help in overcoming the problem of low self-esteem.

Be Your Husband's Cheerleader!

A cheerleader urges and encourages someone to succeed when a difficult or important task is at hand. Holler, holler, girls! A cheerleader whips up energy for concentration and success. Giving ultimatums or a cold shoulder or keeping malice will not bring the best out of your husband. Dear woman, it is self-sabotage to take your husband to the cleaners or give him the venom of your tongue or prove to him that you are better than him.

A very simple yet profound demonstration of cheering one's husband was engraved in my mind during my compulsory National Youth Service days in the old Benue Plateau State of Nigeria. There was this young couple, newly married and posted to camp together. The young man took part in a race during one of the routine physical exercises for corps members, and as he ran, his wife ran with him on the sideline, cheering him all the way to victory. For some reason I have never forgotten this simple act. She ran that race with her husband, just as though she was on the track competing!

When your husband feels weighed down, or even crushed, under the weight of unemployment, financial strain, illness, or disability, you must encourage him and help him back to his feet. Sometimes he may need the refining hand of God in his life; in that case, you have to help him until the work is completed and he becomes a better person. You only have to keep in mind that these changes take time, patience, and commitment.

Your husband must succeed in all areas of his life, and you are the best person on earth to help him put his best into whatever he does and to finish strong. Never give up, even when the expected results are not yet seen. You must keep encouraging your husband to make the right choices and excel in his work and walk with God. If he is discouraged or upset over a problem, you must engage his mind in order to help him. This way, the children have an example to follow in their lives and subsequently in their own homes.

Find Wisdom

Proverbs 4:7 (KJV) says, "Wisdom is the principal thing; get wisdom." This advice is good for everyone, but particularly for the woman who wants to marry a man and have a successful home. Even God made the world by His wisdom; how much more should a woman seek this priceless gift from God. Proverbs 3:18–19 says, "Wisdom is a tree of life to those who eat her fruit; happy is the man who keeps on eating it. The Lord's wisdom founded the earth; his understanding established all the universe and space."

Wisdom is the practical application of knowledge, so a woman should seek knowledge that will enhance her life and that of her family. An English proverb says, "A mother's work is never done." Since the role of a woman is for life, even though it comes in many phases, wisdom is a primary need for every woman. It is wisdom that helps her juggle the many parts she has to play throughout her lifetime. It is by wisdom that she handles grave decisions that may ruin her marriage if not properly handled. It is wisdom that helps her decide when to seek counsel before an issue gets out of hand and ruins her marriage.

If your husband trusts you with information or money, do not mismanage it. If you do, the perception will be created in his mind that you are unreliable or immature. A woman wanted to buy a sports utility vehicle, even though her family already had four other cars for their use. Her husband did not agree with this. She bided her time until her husband traveled, leaving her with the financial mandate for their family business. As soon as she assumed full charge of the finances of the company, she bought the sports utility vehicle without her husband's knowledge. Trouble erupted when her husband returned, and this almost led to the breaking up of their marriage. There was no peace until she sold the SUV. I am sure we do not want to create problems like this in our homes.

It is important that your husband's heart be at peace when he asks you to attend to some issues. He should be able to trust your judgment if decisions have to be made in his absence. If your husband discusses a sensitive issue with you, it should not become a weapon used to taunt him when you have a disagreement, nor should it be made a topic of discussion among your friends.

THOUGHT AND PRAYER

As wisdom is the principal thing, I will seek and pursue it until it is demonstrable in my life, especially in my relationship with my husband and family.

Oh, fountain of wisdom, I ask for Your help to make me a wise woman and to help others to seek You by the way I lead my life. In Jesus' name, amen.

Beneficial Disagreements

Not all disagreements are bad; they may sometimes show that we have more than one way of achieving a goal. We need to learn not to be disagreeable when we disagree with our spouses. Wherever there are two or more people, there will always be some misunderstanding, difference of opinion, or conflict. About the only way to live without ever having an open conflict is to live in isolation, as a hermit, or with one partner becoming a doormat who chooses peace at any price. But none of these situations is actually conflict-free; the conflicts have just gone underground or been redirected.

Mutual presence and respect form the basis for all meaningful relationships. Each person has a point to make and should be able to make it without being rude or demeaning to their partner. No woman should be rude to her husband because of a disagreement or a different point of view on an issue.

In our offices, we have meetings where different ideas are generated through brainstorming and we manage to work together; we can do same at home. I realize the issues we deal with at home may be more emotive and sometimes explosive; yet if we live in an atmosphere of love and trust, we can handle even the toughest issues without our homes falling apart.

When all the points have been made and a final decision is not reached by consensus, a woman should allow her husband to have the last say. Did I hear you say I betrayed the women because they have better intuition? Remember, the man is the head of this team, and where there is difficulty in making decisions, he has the power to work in the interests of the family. Women should prayerfully accept and abide by their husbands' decisions. If we still think a decision may not work in the interests of our family, we can revisit it later, while first abiding by it. A woman should not sabotage her husband's decisions without having them both revisit of the thorny issues. Remember, every couple is in a partnership and they both work for the interests of the family.

No Tantrums and Threats, Please!

If a woman disagrees with her husband over an issue, she should not keep malice with him, give the silent treatment, threaten him, throw tantrums, or move out of her matrimonial home. I have been told that moving out used to be some women's romantic way of getting their husbands to demonstrate their love by coming to get them back into their home. Honestly, I think moving out of the home is a demonstration of ignorance on the part of the woman. The home belongs to both husband and wife, and it is dereliction of duty to move out of it to test your husband's love for you.

A woman should not spend her time and emotions on this; she should spend time planting herself in her husband's heart and mind by demonstrating love for him and their children. It is not in the interest of a woman to control her husband; it reduces his sense of responsibility and commitment to the family.

Instead of taking control, keep helping your husband if he is quiet or tentative in the way he handles issues. Many times, a person can be helped to grow in confidence and take his rightful place in a relationship.

A better known word similar to throwing tantrums is *nagging*. A woman who nags keeps complaining about the same issues without making helpful suggestions to sort them out. If we think through issues together, we often can overcome our differences without damaging our relationships.

When There Is No Child

Sometimes, a couple may find it difficult to bear children, and this may put a strain on the relationship if not properly handled. In an attempt to help or show love to the couple, their relatives and friends may unwittingly add to the stress that goes with waiting for the children to arrive.

In the African setting, unfruitfulness is a landmine for marriages because it often leads to infidelity, distrust, and, in some cases, the breakdown of the marriage. Some Christians are encouraged to patronize witchdoctors and some dubious enchanters and diviners. In extreme cases, the man may be advised to take another wife, as wives are almost always given the blame for unfruitfulness.

With this type of challenge, as with others, it is best to pray, discuss, and seek medical advice if the problem lingers. Delayed conception is usually a very bitter experience for the woman, especially with the many complications that might come from her in-laws. Thankfully, there are many examples in the Bible of barren women giving birth, so we can prayerfully live with the assurance that God will help us while we do all that is needful.

A woman can reduce the stress of unfruitfulness by becoming closer to her husband and doing many things with him to facilitate bonding. A woman in this situation should fight the tendency to start seeing lovemaking as only meant for pro-creation and engaging in it solely for that purpose. This change will be noticed by her husband, and it will affect their relationship.

A woman needs to be in control of her emotions at all times, but especially during trying periods such as this. She must work to make her relationship with her husband as good as always while making herself desirable and fun to be with. I knew a young lady who went on an "orgy of infidelity," going from one man to another because she was "looking for a baby"! This is inexcusable and must be condemned totally.

A Christian woman seeking the fruit of the womb can look at the examples of women in the Bible who passed through this problem and went on to have their own children—women like Sarah (Genesis 18–21), Hannah (1 Samuel 1), and Elizabeth (Luke 1:36–64). Even in our present day, there are many examples of couples who encountered delays in having babies yet did not allow the waiting period to fracture or break their marriage. A certain couple I know waited thirteen years before they had their first baby, and this did not damage their marriage in any way. We will do well to learn from their example.

Indeed, this philosophy can be applied to any problem a couple may face in their marriage. Problems are better handled together in unity and singleness of purpose, keeping the interests of the family on the front burner at all times.

When Your Husband Is Distracted

It is possible for your husband to be distracted, whether you believe this or not. The culprits may range from work to friends, family, and, of course, other women. We tend to think of distraction only in terms of marital infidelity, but other distractions exist and the symptoms are the same—a shift in his interest in you and a flagging commitment. When this is handled with maturity, the balance of the relationship is restored.

As a relationship simmers and settles into a routine, time spent together may be reduced, and every woman would do well to prepare for this. However, this is different from distraction, which is usually a sudden, noticeable lack of interest from your husband in spending time with you. If this happens, all outstanding areas of disagreement must be dealt with in an atmosphere of peace and understanding. Some men handle confrontation well; still, I would advise against taking a confrontational approach at first. That may become necessary when all gentle reminders and promptings have failed. I believe that most of the time, using our intuitive gifts can help restore our relationships without third-party intrusion and other elaborate forms of intervention.

Part Four

Twelve

Relating with Your "New" People

UTH IN THE Bible gave us this very lovely phrase that is sometimes read during the exchange of wedding vows: "Do not ask me to leave you, for I want to go wherever you go, to live wherever you live; your people shall be my people, and your God shall be my God. I want to die where you die, and be buried there" (Ruth 1:16–17).

This very touching account of loyalty is the stuff that total commitment is made of. However, some women find it challenging to accept their husbands' relatives. Every woman must accept her husband's relatives as her own. She must work on making the relationship mutually beneficial and respectful. There is a Yoruba adage that says, "What is acceptable behavior in one family may be

"Resentment is like drinking poison and expecting it to harm your enemy."
— Nelson Mandela

111

frowned upon in another." Every woman must learn what is necessary to build a good relationship among members of her new family.

Africans celebrate marriage as a union between families, as well as between a man and woman. We must work hard to accommodate our new relatives in an atmosphere of love and respect instead of suspicion and distrust. Just as Ruth loved and respected Naomi, her mother-in-law, every woman should respect her mother-in-law and other relatives of her husband. When disagreements occur, the husband should mediate to resolve them amicably. Remember, we trust our husbands to work in our interest. Even if your husband is partial towards his family, you can still present a united front by making this observation to him in private, instead of pulling down the roof because of it. Marriage is a lifelong relationship, and we must commit to it as a work in progress, instead of becoming adversaries of our in-laws.

Dealing With Anger

"A hot-tempered man starts fights and gets into all kinds of trouble," says Proverbs 29:22. Being prone to anger is often due to unresolved issues and can express itself in a score of destructive ways, including resentment, a negative and critical attitude, hostility, and hatred. Anger causes all sorts of problems both to the one who is angry and to those on whom he dumps his anger. Repressed anger can become super-charged and cause the angry person to explode and lash out and hurt people—even murder them. Or it can cause a person to implode, ruin his physical health, and destroy his relationships.

If a man harbors anger at either parent and does not resolve it, he will inevitably take it out on his wife and children. The same applies to every unresolved relational problem from the past. So, to build and sustain a healthy marriage in the present, it is imperative that we resolve the issues in us that were caused by any impaired significant relationship from the past. Unresolved anger has been described as "an emotional cancer, and you either get the 'cancer' or the 'cancer' gets you—one way or another."

Furthermore, angry people are forever looking for pegs to hang their anger on. Instead of facing their own reality, they are constantly looking for faults—real or imagined—in others so they can dump their anger on them and blame them for it. Anger leads to bitterness and resentment. Steve Farrar, an author, said, "Bitterness, like a burning match, only burns the one who holds on to it."[1] The great South African leader Nelson Mandela is said to have explained why he held no bitterness or resentment against those who had imprisoned him during the apartheid regime in his country before he became its first black president. He said, "Resentment is like drinking poison and expecting it to harm your enemy."

If you are petulant and quarrelsome, people will avoid you and you will have few friends. Anger will also break your marriage. There is an adage that says, "A woman without good manners will always complain that other people are not allowing her to enjoy her matrimonial home."

Anger makes people prone to treating others with disrespect. If you have an anger problem, the first thing to do is admit it, ask God to help you find the help you need to resolve it, maintain your relationships, and then seek the help of a qualified counselor. This is one of the most loving things you can do for your loved ones and for yourself. It will be helpful to deal with the underlying problems manifesting as anger. They may include a critical and judgmental spirit, unmet needs, and unfulfilled expectations, amongst others.

If you are not prone to anger but have to deal with someone who is, ask God to give you the courage to lovingly confront them, letting them know that you will no longer allow them to treat you disrespectfully and that you will have to distance yourself from them if they refuse to get the help they need to overcome their anger issues.

There's a story of a lady of privilege who cut off a great part of her hair after a quarrel with her husband. She then asked an artist to paint her with her new hairstyle, with her holding the clump of cut hair. By doing this, she immortalized the quarrel and it went into the annals of that marriage's history! Was that really necessary? Sometimes we have to let things go; so many of us are clutching at the remnants of issues that need to be forgotten.

A related issue to anger is envy or

jealousy. Dr. Chris Kwakpovwe, author of the devotional *Our Daily Manna*, describes envy in a very apt manner. He says, "Envy is the art of counting other people's blessings instead of your own." If envy meant just counting other people's blessings, it could be as harmless as being a busybody; but the envious person goes further to make her life unhappy and has vicious thoughts towards the object of her jealousy. An English proverb says, "Envy shoots at others and wounds itself." Envy always wounds itself and must be dealt with. Immature people are usually unsure of themselves, and in comparing themselves with their successful friends, become envious. If you know the purpose of your being here on earth and are working toward its fulfillment, you will be less likely to envy others.

Don't Give God Orders!

Remember, God is in a relationship too—with you! If you make a habit of issuing Him orders to perform or get out of your life, you may be courting trouble for yourself and those dear to you. If there are problems, by all means hold God to His words, especially if you are in a relationship with Him. This, however, does not include ordering Him to perform: "God, perform or I quit serving You!" That is the most frustrating thing you can do to yourself.

If you can develop to the level of not requiring confirmation of your worth, how much more can God! He remains God whether He answers your prayer as you would like or not. Some of us are so good at threatening people to get our way and may unknowingly extend this to our relationship with God. An understanding of God's

Word and His ways will be beneficial to us in all our relationships.

THOUGHT AND PRAYER

I can deal with issues I am not pleased with by being calm enough to hear the other side, and I will not allow jealousy or envy into my life because I know God's purpose for my life and am committed to it. I will work to establish a relationship with God that will make the will of God the government of my life and the glory of God the reason for my life.

Oh, Lord, thank You as I make the best of what I have and align myself with Your will. In Jesus' name, amen.

Is a Woman a Victim in Marriage?

> People who consider themselves victims of their circumstances will always remain victims unless they develop a greater vision for their lives.
>
> —STEDMAN GRAHAM[2]

It may be instructive to know how many people, especially women, think they are victims in their marriages. Many may well believe their lives would have turned out better if they had not gotten married; in other words, they are victims of marriage.

Every woman planning to get married must have it clear in her mind that she will not be a victim in her marriage or a victim of marriage. There is no doubt that a woman gives more to make a house a home and a marriage successful, but this does not in any way make her a slave or a victim. It is entirely up to a woman to decide what she brings into a marriage that her husband will love and enjoy while respecting her.

I found the piece below on the Internet and decided to include it as an example of how not to handle your marital problems:

> When I got home that night as my wife served dinner, I held her hand and said, "I've got something to tell you." She sat down and ate quietly. Again I observed the hurt in her eyes. Suddenly I didn't know how to open my mouth. But I had to let her know what I was thinking. I want a divorce. I raised the topic calmly...
>
> In the morning, she presented her divorce conditions: she didn't want anything from me but needed a month's notice before the divorce.
>
> She requested that in that one month, we both struggle to live as normal a life as possible. Her reasons were simple: Our son had his exams in a month's time, and she didn't want to disrupt him with our broken marriage...
>
> My wife and I hadn't had any body contact since my divorce intention was explicitly expressed. So when I carried

her out on the first day, we both appeared clumsy...

But her much lighter weight made me sad...

I drove to office and jumped out of the car swiftly without locking the door. I was afraid any delay would make me change my mind. I walked upstairs. Dew opened the door and I said to her, "Sorry, Dew. I do not want the divorce anymore."...

At the floral shop on the way, I ordered a bouquet of flowers for my wife. The salesgirl asked me what to write on the card. I smiled and wrote, *I'll carry you out every morning until death do us apart.*

That evening I arrived home, flowers in my hands, a smile on my face; I run up stairs, only to find my wife in the bed—dead.[3]

The lesson from this sad story is that we need help sometimes and we need to have helpful relationships that can bail us out of dire situations. Please do not keep a problem to yourself to the point where it drives you mad or even kills you. Live and help your husband; do not die because of him! There is help somewhere nearby; it could be through your church or in form of a mature godly woman to whom you can unburden your heart. Every heart has a carrying capacity for problems, and if exceeded, there will be trouble. Do not allow your heart to carry undue burdens, and do not die of a broken heart.

THOUGHT AND PRAYER

I am wonderfully made by God and endowed with all that I need to be a fulfilled woman and wife. I will not be a victim in my relationships. I am capable of making decisions in favor of myself, my husband, and family, and I intend to do this every time.

Dear Lord, please help me use the resources You have endowed me with to the best interest of myself, my husband, and family. In Jesus' name, amen.

Thirteen

Healing Choices for Life

As Nancy Leigh DeMoss writes, "The grateful heart that springs forth in joy is not acquired in a moment; it is the fruit of a thousand choices."[1] Was your heart broken in a previous relationship and you are wondering if it will happen again? You have a choice in this matter. As another has said:

> "The grateful heart that springs forth in joy is not acquired in a moment; it is the fruit of a thousand choices."
>
> —Nancy Leigh DeMoss

> Our lives are not determined by what happens to us but how we react to what happens; not by what life brings to us but by the attitude we bring to life. A positive attitude causes a chain reaction of positive thoughts,

"It's easy to carry the past as a burden instead of a school. It's easy to let it overwhelm you instead of educate you."
—Jim Rohn

events, and outcomes. It is a catalyst…a spark that creates extraordinary results.

—Anonymous[2]

You can learn from the past and move on by not dwelling on its painful details and ability to harm you. A philosopher once said that life has pains and the only way to deal with them is to go through them quickly. The more we dwell on the hurt, the greater its power to harm us.

Our issues as women are usually quite similar. I know a beautiful young lady who had two previous bad relationships and is very suspicious of men. She lives under the shadow of those relationships. I want to admonish everyone, as I admonished her, to let the past pass. I said to her, "The past is past; let us learn from it and move on to the future."

When the past gives them a raw deal, the tendency of many women is to be hostile to men, believing they are all bad and unreliable. Jim Rohn, an American business philosopher, said: "It's easy to carry the past as a burden instead of a school. It's easy to let it overwhelm you instead of educate you."

To worsen the problem, people tend to

attract other people who think like them; this has a way of reinforcing the negative thoughts they have and worsening the problem. In fact, the issue of past baggage is now certified as a problem and not just a challenge. People respond to challenges better than they do to problems; they have the emotional resources to face challenges but are knocked down by problems.

"Good friends are good for your health."
—Irwin Sarason

The way I see it, a challenge brings out the best in you that you can apply to the issue, while a problem may leave you bewildered and at the end of your wits. It is necessary to classify our issues in relationships as challenges so we can prayerfully muster the strength to overcome them. Some women believe their lives should be one long party without any challenges. It is important that they change this mindset. While we do not go in search of challenges, we need them in order to grow and become better, so we should see them as a means to improve ourselves. Our emotional well-being will improve significantly if we do not shy away from challenges but rise up to each one with our God-given emotional resources and our network of other relationships.

Dear diva, what is the use of your sense of self-worth and poise if it depends on circumstances? Our self-worth must flow from what God has said about us in the Bible. We must also use our network of friends effectively to help us in time of need.

Be sure to share your friends' challenges, as well. When they succeed, be pleased and rejoice with them; when they mourn, genuinely mourn with them. This is important so we can keep a healthy network of people that we can share our burdens with.

> Good friends are good for your health.
> —IRWIN SARASON[3]

Choose life and celebrate your recovery from past challenges by seeing with the eyes of faith. Of course, lessons must be learned from past mistakes so they are not repeated, but you must not keep on beating yourself up or stumbling over the same sad issue.

Disruptive Attraction

A person can be attracted in an unwholesome sense to other objects, and this can lead to a disruption of his or her life. For the purpose of this book, I will describe two categories of disruptive attraction.

Disruptive attraction to material things

The Bible in 1 John 2:15–16 (KJV) talks about the lust of the flesh, lust of the eyes, and the pride of life, and this can apply to men as well as women:

> Love not the world, neither the things that are in the world. If any man love the world, the love of the Father is not in him.

> For all that is in the world, the lust of
> the flesh, and the lust of the eyes, and the
> pride of life, is not of the Father, but is of
> the world.

The "world" referred to in the passage is not the earth but a belief system and the act of making decisions without recourse to the purpose of God. A person cannot be called worldly simply because they dress well or are fashionable.

This book is written primarily for women, so I will dwell on the attraction to material things as it relates to women. There is a general belief that women love things like gold and diverse items of jewelry, expensive clothes and cars and flashy things, while they pay little attention to investments and planning for the future. This general perception is not always true, yet it seems so with many women and this makes it necessary to discuss this.

Some men do not allow their wives know how much they earn or do not tell them if they come into a substantial amount of wealth because they believe she will squander the money. Women must work hard to change this perception. The urge to acquire things just for the sake of having them must be tamed in every woman who will earn her husband's respect and trust.

This is the age of *aso-ebi* (uniform, often expensive dress for special occasions, such as weddings and child dedications), and even the church has not been spared this trend. In itself, identifying with friends and family on these occasions is commendable, yet the expenses may be too high for the average family to bear and may put a young family in financial distress if wisdom is not applied. Once this habit starts, it is difficult to put a stop to it without offending your friends. It may be good to sometimes decline if you have clothes that match the color code for the special occasion. Many women's expenses exceed their income, yet they cannot afford to say no to the next *aso-ebi*, especially when the celebrant has already taken the liberty of packaging and sending it to her!

We all must cultivate the habit of allowing others their own opinions and judgment when the issue of committing funds to such occasions arises. Some women buy things just because they can afford them and not because they are needed. There are yet others whose source of joy is spending money. They are unhappy and bored when they are not shopping or spending money. We need to watch out for such tendencies so they do not become a disruptive attraction.

Some women are revelers, never at ease when they are not attending parties and other social engagements. It is not wrong to attend social gatherings, but if a person's life is taken over by these events, they could become disruptive to family life. A woman must enjoy living and still have a sense of moderation in all things. No one can prescribe for another person the number of social engagements that are adequate, but each person can judge for themselves when they are doing something in excess or when their spouse begins to complain. A word to the Christian woman who spends seven days in church every week of the month: you could be guilty of allowing a disruptive attraction, especially if your children are left to roam around or left in the care of neighbors. The Spirit of the Lord will teach us wisdom in all things. If we judge ourselves, the Bible says we will not be judged (1 Cor. 11:31).

Disruptive attraction to people, especially of the opposite sex

Any time a woman is so attracted to a person that it negatively affects her family, she may be falling into disruptive behavior. It is a woman's duty to guard her affections.

There is also a form of disruptive attraction that a woman can get into when she is attracted to a man who abuses her mentally and/or physically. There are single ladies who choose to stay in disruptive relationships because they are afraid they will not find another man to marry them. Some stay on in these relationships because they think the man loves them or that they love him. A woman must think deeply and examine her sense of worth; if she finds herself staying in an abusive relationship, there is most likely something wrong with her self-worth.

Any man who claims to be a Christian and yet abuses his wife verbally or physically needs urgent deliverance from the devil and his wiles. I read the story of a woman who was a victim of abuse from her husband for many years, even though he claimed to be a church-going Christian. She was advised to endure this situation for so many years, and she became a nervous wreck. No woman should expose herself to abuse from anyone, and definitely not from someone who claims to love her. This topic shall be further examined later on in this book.

Deal With Entanglements

It is important to deal with all forms of entanglements before marriage. All relationships of an amorous nature, with people outside of one's spouse, must be cut off before marriage to give it (the marriage) a chance to grow. Entanglements can be, for this purpose, categorized into two—there are internal entanglements, which are entanglements with your own problems; and external entanglements, which involve other people's problems. Do not take any man as your "project" by trying to fix or change him.

Do Not Lead Yourself Into Temptation

Just about anyone can fall into temptation if he or she yields to its allure. A person can only be tempted by something they find attractive; if something isn't attractive to you, then it's not a temptation for you. Eve in the Bible admitted that the forbidden fruit was good for food, pleasant to the eyes, and desirable to make one wise before she ate it (Genesis 3).

The promise a temptation offers is very compelling and fuels the longing to have it. It is similar to the power of advertising, where products are linked to concepts and lifestyles of success. There is always something desirable and compelling about the object of temptation, but the power to resist is available to every person. Sometimes we blame others for leading us into temptation, but we are in fact to blame when we give people the permission to lead us there.

Because of the powerful nature of temptation, the Bible advises us not to yield to it; also in fact, we are advised to "flee" from lust (1 Cor. 6:18). If you happen to meet an old boyfriend, be sure not to fan the embers of your lost love! You have moved on and, if you are married, made a choice; please stay true to your vows.

Avoid emotional infidelity, which, when it has grown, will lead to sexual infidelity. Anyone seeking to commit adultery with you knows that your pleas of "This is wrong" are half-hearted and will brush it aside and take advantage of your vulnerability. Know your boundaries up front, and keep them by avoiding compromising situations. Help your husband by noticing his weaknesses, and help him avoid those situations. As long as you keep meeting men—and this is bound to happen—you risk being tempted, so you have to be on your guard always. Marriage is a lifelong commitment.

A woman is tempted mostly by the things she hears from a man, while a man is more affected by the things he sees in a woman. You need to apply wisdom in dealing with sensitive issues, both on your own part and in helping your husband overcome his own attractions.

THOUGHT AND PRAYER

I have the capability to make wise and healing choices in life, especially in my marriage. I will always use this capacity as I lead my life and interact with others, especially in my marriage.

Dear Lord, thank You for grace upon my life to make healthy and healing choices as the needs arise. Help me keep this before me at all times. In Jesus' name, amen.

Vows, Covenants, and Allegiances

I have attempted to set out simple explanations for these three words below, especially as they relate to marriage. Christians are promise-keepers, yet sometimes they find themselves at odds when they enter into marriage. We must stop bandying words whose meanings we do not know or are not committed to keeping.

In her article, "The Unraveling of a Christian Marriage: Why I Stayed," Elisabeth Corcoran has this to say:

> I promised God I would stay. I told myself innumerable times over the years that the only reason I was staying was because I told God I would. I made a promise, a vow. I entered into a covenant. I don't take that lightly. I want to be the kind of person that people count on, that *God* can count on. I stayed because God is my authority, the One I will answer to, and the thought of disappointing him broke my heart on a regular basis.[4]

Now, that is what I call commitment and an understanding of vows and covenants!

Vows

A vow is a binding promise or pledge. We take a marriage vow during our wedding, and it is binding on the two persons concerned as long as they are both alive. The marriage vow is a promise to have and to hold in all situations—for better or worse—till death. It is a very deep vow that is modeled on the relationship between Jesus Christ and the church. It is a promise to stay true to one another and to share life's twists and turns together. If we stay true to our marriage vows, we are better positioned to get the best out of our challenges and to improve our marriages. As renewal is a strong and positive thing, we can renew our wedding vows from time to time as a reminder to help us work on our relationship.

In Judges 11:30–37, the story is told of a vow made to the Lord by Jephthah. Jephthah promised that if God would give him victory over the Ammonites, he would sacrifice as a burnt offering the first person to meet him when he arrived home after the war. God accepted this and gave Jephthah victory. As he returned home, it was his only daughter who came out to rejoice with him over his victory. Jephthah had to keep his vow, but with a very painful heart.

Also, Hannah, the mother of Samuel, made a vow that if the Lord answered her request and gave her a son, she would give him back to the Lord (1 Sam. 1:11). She kept her vow, as we see in 1 Samuel 1:26–28.

When we make a vow, we are to keep it (Deut. 23:21).

Covenants

A covenant is a mutual agreement or contract between persons, or between God and humanity. It has conditions and consequences that are spelled out.

We know God's covenant with Abraham, and many of us are still claiming Abraham's blessings even today, generations after the covenant was made. We also know the covenant of God with mankind through the blood of Jesus.

It is through this that salvation became available to us.

Covenants in the Bible usually involved blood and were deeply sacred. Marriage is sacred covenant, too, and it involves the mixing of blood also, so it must not be taken lightly. The "stolen water is sweet" mentality must be done away with among Christians. Sex is a covenant act within marriage and must be treated with care and commitment, not as a common or dirty act. The power of covenants can be harnessed through generations as we commit to our marriages and relationships.

Allegiances

Allegiances are partnerships that are binding and have conditions and consequences. A lesser person may give allegiance as a form of commitment to the greater. Human beings give their allegiance to God as an act of worship. The Christian family will benefit from its allegiance to the Lord Jesus Christ. We can pledge allegiance to the Lamb of God. It is a commitment to service. In my family, we pray often, giving our allegiance to Jesus Christ, and I want to commend that you do the same.

Deliverances

Deliverance is being set free from the consequences of our negative actions or other people's actions taken on our behalf. Deliverance may be appropriate on account of what we do wrong in handling our vows, covenants, and allegiances. Any married man or woman who ever slept with any person apart from his or her spouse is in need of deliverance. Any man or woman who has roving eyes and lives under the guilt of constant lust needs deliverance.

What I am trying to explain is that we all need deliverance if we are to keep healthy marriage relationships. This book is not written to accuse anyone; it is to give suggestions on how to move our marriages forward, loving our husbands with all of our hearts and possessions.

There are occurrences in our relationships and families that arise directly from issues we need deliverance from. You can apply self-deliverance by the Word of God on your life and on the lives of your family members. Psalm 51 readily comes to mind as a good example of self-deliverance made by David.

Self-deliverance does not mean one is delivering oneself; it means one is applying the Word of God for one's own deliverance. Where you are unable to apply deliverance on your own, please seek your pastor's counsel. The institution of marriage is under such serious attack that no stone must be left unturned in dealing with these issues.

THOUGHT AND PRAYER

I pledge allegiance to the Lord Jesus Christ and His cause in all things. I will walk in line with His Word and make amends if I fall short of His laws. I apply the cleansing blood of Jesus to my family.

Dear Father, thank You for giving us all things that are needed for life and holy living. By Your grace, we will be true to our vows and covenants. Help us as we take advantage of Your provision for deliverance. In Jesus' name, amen.

Beware of Love That Costs You Nothing!

> The influence a woman has with her husband is a sacred trust to be guarded and used in the interest of the family and God, who instituted marriage.

King David said in the Bible that he would not give God something that cost him nothing (1 Chron. 21:24). Love is about relationships, and if love costs you nothing, then it is mercenary. If every adjustment or change to be made for the success of your marriage is made by only one person, then that love is mercenary. When a woman boasts that she can order her husband around like he has no will or opinion of his own, her love is mercenary. The influence a woman has with her husband is a sacred trust to be guarded and used in the interest of the family and God, who instituted marriage. Any other use of this influence is an abuse and it is dangerous. The day a man realizes he is being used is the day trust is damaged in your relationship and your influence lost. You will cease to get his cooperation on issues as quickly as you used to; he will begin to weigh all options, looking out for pitfalls and trying to discern your hidden agenda. This is not in the interest of any woman, and definitely not in the interest of the family.

It is now a common belief among many women that they should not contribute to or go out of their way to make sacrifices that would lead to a man's success, so as to avoid disappointment later on in the relationship. This belief has led many women to seek out men they consider successful or rich when they want to get married. There is nothing wrong with marrying a rich or successful man, but this should not be the most important qualification a man has before he is considered suitable for marriage.

A woman should make her marriage her top priority while encouraging activities that strengthen the bond between her and her husband. A woman, by nature, nurtures and gives; this is where her blessing, honor, and uplifting lie. If we successfully impress upon our husbands' hearts that we love them, they will work in our favor most of the time, and the few times they may make mistakes can be dealt with through dialogue and prayers. A woman is to love her husband whether he is lovely, lovable, or unlovable. We can create a design of what we want our families to be through prayer and planning together.

Part Five

Fourteen

Honoring Lappidoth

T HERE IS A piece of scripture I find fascinating: Judges
4:4. It talks about Deborah, one of Israel's judges at
the time. It says, "Israel's leader at that time, the
one who was responsible for bringing the people back to
God, was Deborah, a prophetess, the wife of Lappidoth."
The following verses describe how Deborah carried out
her duties as a judge.

What I find fascinating about the verse above is the
descriptive phrase "the wife of Lappidoth" in relation to
Judge Deborah. In my study of the Bible over time, I have
not come across the name Lappidoth in any other verse;
yet it was important to describe Deborah in terms of her
marriage. This means that Lappidoth was known and
recognized in their time. He must have had his own area
of influence.

If Deborah had not been a judge in Israel at that
time, Lappidoth may never have been mentioned in the
Bible. There is nothing to suggest that Lappidoth was not
an important member of his society, but it was his wife,

139

Deborah, who held a defining position among the judges in Israel at that time.

The lesson here is that your position in society as a woman does not reduce the importance of your marriage partner. The importance of your husband is not determined by his high-level position in government or industry. A woman must honor her husband, whatever level of achievement she attains in society. This should not be done merely for public show, but also in their private lives. Deborah was a judge in a male-dominated society, yet she was married; so your level of achievement should not be a limiting factor to a successful marriage. Women should work at making their marriages a very important and defining part of their lives, such as it was for Deborah.

Please allow me introduce to you an accomplished lawyer and judge (maybe a modern-day Deborah!), Honourable Justice Olatokunbo Olopade, wife of Duro Jimi "DJ" Olopade, himself an accomplished businessman and retired public servant. Justice Olopade is my childhood friend, a schoolmate from Queen's School Ede/Ibadan, and a scion of the Odumosu family of Ijebu Ayepe in Ogun State. Her illustrious father, Mr. Peter Taiwo Odumosu, along with his very fashionable wife of many years, Mrs. Victoria Odumosu, was one of the earliest staunch Christians in the then Western region of Nigeria. In the early 1970s, when the wave of commitment to the lordship of Jesus Christ hit our land, Mr. P. T. Odumosu was one of the older people who was committed to Christ and remained steadfast until death. He was a shining example to all the young Christians who were looking for role models in those early days. He was also the head of the Civil Service and Secretary to the military government of the pace-setting Western State of Nigeria in those days of highly disciplined public servants.

I have gone into this detail so you can have a peek into the privileged background of our diva, Olatokunbo. She and her husband have been married for thirty-four years now. Her husband is successful and ever so supportive of his wife's success, and their marriage has been a beautiful one. The great Christian heritage bequeathed to her by her parents has paid off by her becoming a celebrated, virtuous woman. She combined a successful career with a good and enduring marriage. She was recently made the Chief Judge of Ogun State of Nigeria. We congratulate and commend her to all women as a worthy model in conduct and commitment to God. Pass on the torch, Toks!

THOUGHT AND PRAYER

I will love and respect my husband, even when I have attained prominence and fame in career or business. I will bequeath a great Christian heritage to my children.

Lord, thank You for the Christian heritage I have. I ask for grace to pass it on to my children and lineage. In Jesus' name, amen.

Fifteen

Some Lessons Ladies Must Learn

A S THE SAYING goes, "If we keep doing what we've always done, we'll keep getting what we've always got, and we'll keep feeling what we've always felt." In other words, if we want to bring about change, whether in our personal lives, families, businesses, churches, or nation, we need to look at things differently and be prepared to make changes—sometimes drastic changes! Without change, nothing ever changes. The woman, the Christian woman included, needs to take a look at her life and make the necessary changes that will help her become a better person as a wife, mother, friend, and so on.

Without change, nothing ever changes.

143

Relate, Don't Retaliate

When my pastor, Rev. Idowu Akintola, said in one of his sermons, "Relate, do not react," it struck a chord in my heart as wise counsel. Of course, both men and women need to take this advice to heart, but I want to specially urge women to work on this. Please do not settle scores or retaliate when there is a problem or you have been hurt. Many times, we (men and women alike) react to people based on the perception that we need to defend ourselves or our points of view. When this happens, we take on the attitudes expressed in some of the clichés we use or come across in our everyday lives: "fire for fire," "You do me, I do you," "I am ready for anything," "Fight to the finish," "If a bird cannot have the seeds, it will waste them so no one else can eat them," and so on.

Retaliating breeds resentment, especially if you feel outclassed or outmaneuvered in spite of your strong points. The best way to relate to any matter at hand is to understand the issues as well as the other person's point of view. You may also state your own opinion and then iron out the differences. No woman should make her home a battlefield or a theatre for intrigue and politics. Comportment is very important, so every woman must comport herself in a way that will earn the respect of her husband. There is, however, no justification for any man to beat his wife, no matter the provocation. As women, if we relate instead of retaliating when challenges occur, we may resolve issues amicably and promote harmonious relationships in our homes, and even the wider society.

Lessons From Trees

> All those who listen to my instructions
> and follow them are wise, like a man who
> builds his house on solid rock.
> Though the rain comes in torrents, and
> the flood rises and the storm winds beat
> against the house, it won't collapse, for it is
> built on rock.
> But those who hear my instructions and
> ignore them are foolish, like a man who
> builds his house on sand.
> For when the rains and floods come, and
> storm winds beat against his house, it will
> fall with a mighty crash.
> —MATTHEW 7:24–27

I have had to visit Jos, the Plateau State capital in Nigeria, very often in the last three years. On one of such visits, I noticed many trees, felled by a terrible rainstorm the previous day. I was surprised by this significant observation: While many of the trees themselves were huge and very tall, their roots were unbelievably shallow. I marveled at this inexplicable disproportion, believing that all big trees should have commensurately deep roots. My hostess explained that many of the trees had been exposed to soil erosion for years (probably decades), thus exposing more and more of their roots to the vagaries of the weather and to death. I believe this explanation because I noticed the gullies and the bad state of the roads in the area.

This sort of thing can happen in our lives if our

foundations are faulty—if we do not pay adequate attention to the development of our character and the application of the Word of God in our lives. We must build good and strong foundations for our lives and our marriages and other important relationships. Build your life on a relationship with God through His Son, Jesus Christ. Seek out someone who shares this relationship with God and, together, build your marriage on love, commitment, integrity, and trust so that it will stand the test of life's storms and problems.

You can contrast trees with shallow roots with the gum trees growing in the dry parts of the world, where they are forced to drive their roots down deep in order to survive. Their branches get broken in storms, but rarely do any of the trees fall. This shows us how we should handle challenges, no matter how difficult. In order to survive the storms of life, we need to develop a deep root system that is anchored solidly in our faith in God—the one in whom we trust implicitly.

My pastor, Rev. Idowu Akintola, once said, "Problems determine your fortitude factor." The way you handle problems shows the stuff you are made of! To move you higher still, consider the words of

Ralph Waldo Emerson: "Do not go where the path may lead; go instead where there is no path and leave a trail."

A writer, Richard Innes, had this to say about planting trees when he lived in South Australia at the top of the Adelaide Hills, a windy place. He was advised to plant his trees while they were still small and not to stake them too tightly. He said, "They needed the freedom to bend and sway with the wind, as this helped them develop a deep root system from their beginning, in order to strengthen them when they had fully grown."[1]

Our relationships need freedom to grow, so we should not smother our partners. We can give them some space without harming our marriages. We need not demand to know their every movement or insist on going everywhere with them. Please, do not send investigators or friends to stalk your husband. Give him love and trust, and prayerfully let him grow into his God-given purpose. We should still keep a prayerful lookout for our spouses, but not because we want to accuse them or spy on them. Remember, you cannot force a man to be faithful to you and respect his marriage vows; it is a decision he must take as you show him love and demonstrate your commitment and trust.

> **"Do not go where the path may lead; go instead where there is no path and leave a trail."**
> — **Ralph Waldo Emerson**

Every man loves a woman he can depend on and trust—a loyal partner and a formidable ally.

Dick Innes also wrote about the mighty redwood trees with their leafy arms spread toward the heavens. Normally, they receive good rains, have a sufficient water supply, and grow in groves. These giants of the forest also have a very shallow root system, but as they grow in groves, all their roots are intertwined. When the wild winds blow and the storms rage, they hang on to each other and hold each other up. Women need to cultivate other healthy relationships that can be beneficial in challenging times. And, like the mighty redwoods, if we want to grow strong and healthy we need the support of one another.

Live by the Word of God

Some women avoid facing facts because they find them too threatening, or they may not be able to pay the price to deal with these facts. Others don't face reality because it's not in agreement with or does not go down well with their feelings. Of course, we have to acknowledge our feelings, but we cannot always trust them. There are times we just need to face facts, hold ourselves together, grit our teeth, and do as the Bible says regardless of our feelings. It is much wiser and in our interest to trust God's Word rather than our feelings, just like it would be foolish to be driving on a highway and disregard a warning sign that says "Danger Ahead" because we don't feel the sign is correct or we are not in the mood to obey it that day.

We have considered the place of maturity in conducting our affairs and in our relationships. A mature woman recognizes her feelings, checks them against reality, and doesn't allow them to control her. If our feelings don't align with God's Word, we are better off following God's Word rather than making our feelings the voice of authority. Our feelings can be a very dangerous path to follow, especially when it comes to eternal life and timeless principles and values.

The Word of God has instructions for daily living, and we must learn the principles and live by them in all areas of our lives and relationships. Sometimes it is easier to run from one church to another in search of miracles, when all we need do is live by the precepts of the Word of God. A philosopher once said, "Harmony in sound is music; harmony in color is art; harmony in life is the kingdom of God." We need harmony in life to be better people, good wives, and great mothers.

I keep going back to individual development because you cannot give love when there is no harmony in your life. If you are tossed to and fro by circumstances that you have not come to grips with, it becomes difficult to meet another person's need for love and attention. It is also of no benefit to acquire more knowledge unless you first take action on what you know already. Oswald Chambers, a man of God from centuries past, said, "Never try

> If our feelings don't align with God's Word, we are better off following God's Word rather than making our feelings the voice of authority. Our feelings can be a very dangerous path to follow, especially when it comes to eternal life and timeless principles and values.

to explain God until you've obeyed Him. The only part of God we understand is the part we have obeyed."

Lessons From the Ants

Let's see what valuable lessons we can learn from the ants. For one thing, ants teach performance. Ants are always busy, never lazy, and they never have to make excuses. Our failure to learn this lesson can be evidenced in our slackness toward doing God's work, even as we busy ourselves with television, video games, and the Internet. Our attention can easily be diverted from God's work—including keeping our families—and before we know it the time is gone, the opportunity is lost, and nothing of God's will have been accomplished!

Lessons From Sports

Practice discipline in all aspects of your life. Be prepared for both pleasure and pain. Sportsmen and women discipline themselves to earn medals or financial rewards, which cannot be compared with the worth of a person or a family. In the first letter of Paul to the Corinthians, he compared the preparation of the sportsman or athlete to that of the Christian, enjoining Christians to discipline themselves (1 Cor. 9:25). I urge all women to plan ahead for their careers, marriages, and raising a family. Prayerfully planning ahead is very important factor in making a success of your life. In an age where most women work and are in highly demanding careers, it is important to plan and make decisions on how to work for the success of their families. In planning for a family, it is important to decide beforehand the number of children a couple can effectively care for.

You Are a Priest Too!

The woman is also a priest in the family, and should give prayer cover to the man and the children. The man is the head of the home, and every woman must keep that before her as she works for the uplifting of her family. You must believe in the priesthood of the believer—both male and female. Marriage does not undermine your priesthood as a woman (Exod. 19:6; 1 Pet. 2:5, 9; Rev. 5:10; 20:6). The home does not need only one priest; it needs priests. The home, in fact, benefits from having many priests who are aware of and alive to their responsibilities. As soon as the children are old enough, they are to be led to a commitment to the Lord Jesus Christ, and then they too become priests!

This matter of priesthood in the home is not one to be forced, argued about, or drummed into a man's brain; rather, it is to be grasped, understood, and demonstrated in the interest of the family. Some believe the man is the priest in the house just because the wife is asked to submit. A home needs as many priests as it can get. A priest carries the prayers of the people (family) to God.

151

You need self-awareness to be your best gift to your husband and children.

Please do not define a whole lifetime by one Bible verse; understand the issue, the context of the message, and the trend. Be a robust student of the Bible, taking it in context for better understanding and impact, asking for help from mentors and of course the Holy Spirit, who is the Teacher.

Self-Awareness

You need self-awareness to be your best gift to your husband and children. Self-awareness does not make you haughty or cause you to look down on others; it is a quiet assurance of who God has called you to be. Some women are totally unaware of who they are, so they spend valuable time struggling to be who they are not. This can lead to a lot of envy, anger, and frustration in their lives. As we become aware of who we are, we become free to be ourselves and play our roles better than we ever did before. The starting point to wholeness is self-discovery, and we would all do well to pay attention to this. We have examined this in the section on developing a sense of self-worth.

What God Has Joined Together

When your girlfriend comes ranting and raving about the lack of consideration shown to her by her husband and how very upset and tired she is of his bad behavior, please listen and calm her down. If you say anything negative about her husband, you might have to eat those words when they make up and have settled their differences. I know a lady who had this habit of running to her parents' house to report her husband to them and her siblings whenever they had misunderstandings. Her siblings would insult and say all manner of uncomplimentary things about her husband, but to their chagrin she would rise in defense of her husband, saying, "He is not as bad as that!" Over time, her family learned not to take her complaints about her husband seriously.

Your girlfriend may just want to get things off her chest, so do not join her in running down her husband. Some other perspective may help her see the issue in a better light.

You Can Stick Together for the Long Haul!

Herbert and Zelmyra Fisher of North Carolina in the United States of America have been married eighty-six years and hold the Guinness World Record for the longest marriage of a living couple. Zelmyra is 101 years old, and Herbert is 104. Enjoy the advice given by the couple:

> **Q.** What was the best piece of marriage advice you ever received?

A. Respect, support, and communicate with each other. Be faithful, honest, and true. Love each other with ALL of your heart.

Q. At the end of a bad relationship day, what is the most important thing to remind yourselves?

A. Remember marriage is not a contest—never keep score. God has put the two of you together on the same team to win.

Q. Is fighting important?

A. NEVER physically! Agree that it's okay to disagree, and fight for what really matters. Learn to bend, not break!

Q. What's the one thing you have in common that transcends everything else?

A. We are both Christians and believe in God. Marriage is a commitment to the Lord. We pray with and for each other every day.

Q. You got married very young. How did you both manage to grow as individuals yet not grow apart as a couple?

A. Everyone who plants a seed and harvests the crop celebrates together. We are individuals but accomplish more together.[2]

Everyone who plants a seed and harvests the crop celebrates together. We are individuals but accomplish more together.

Give Him Time to Think

Have you ever discussed a certain matter with your husband and impatiently waited for his input so a decision could be made? In frustration, when he is not forthcoming, you may ask, "Won't you say something?" Then he may say, "You have just told me now, and I have to think about it."

Because women process information differently than men, this may be frustrating for you. But if your husband needs time to think through issues before making suggestions, please give him time. Try to bring up issues for discussion ahead of time, before they become crucial, so there will be no urgency or pressure on him to take a position. You may also gain better perspective from giving him detailed information that may enhance his decision-making. It will help keep your sanity, as well as his.

Also, you may break a conversation for some minutes and later want to pick up the thread and continue it; but to the man, it may seem an altogether different discussion instead of a continuation of what was being said before the break. We would do well as women to note these differences in perception between men and women. They do not make one sex better than the other partner, however; we were made that way to complement each other.

THOUGHT AND PRAYER

I affirm that I am a builder and an encourager. I will not pull anyone down or rejoice when people around me are in distress. I will always lend a helping hand as much as it lies within my power to do so. I will not allow my feelings to override good judgment and timeless principles.

Dear God, thank You for my friends and family and for grace to always be available to help them in all situations, in line with Your word and will. Please help me to always be aware of my feelings, to acknowledge and accept them, express them appropriately whenever necessary, but never allow them to control me. Thank You for hearing and answering my prayer. In Jesus' name, amen.

Panacea for Recalcitrant Behavior

Some behaviors exhibited by your husband may be described as recalcitrant if they are bad and repeated admonition and prayers have not yet yielded any positive change. These will possibly be sources of disagreement and annoyance to you. Identify this behavior and try to isolate it so it does not cloud your judgment of the man and affect your relationship negatively. Once identified and isolated, this behavior should be committed to prayer, and you may have to learn to live with it while the Lord works on him.

When I speak of recalcitrant behavior here, I am referring to new or previously undetected bad behavior that was not identified during courtship. If you identify any behavior while in courtship that you cannot live with, you should rethink marrying the man. Please, do not marry a man you plan to change; it will only lead to nagging and other problems. Do not take any man as a "project"; it will only open the doors of pain and frustration in your marriage. Some single women marry men and regard them as their "cross" to carry throughout their lives. This idea is not of God. The burden we are asked to bear is not to knowingly put ourselves at risk by choosing to marry men without a conscience and commitment to God. Only desperate women do this, and marriage should not be entered into out of desperation. We may need to hone our decision-making capacity and be brutally frank with ourselves in making important decisions. In addition to the input of others who care about us, we need the capacity for "self-talk" as we face difficult challenges. Self-talk is both a call to order and an affirmation in line with God's Word and timeless principles.

The Displacement Syndrome

If you have done all that is possible and some members of your new family are still not pleased with you, please give them room. You may have to live with accusations, such as squandering their son's or brother's wealth. This should not cause any bad blood between you and them if you manage your relationship with them well; some of these feelings ease off over time. At the heart of such accusations is the belief that you have "displaced" them by robbing them of their son's or brother's affection and attention.

This problem of family members feeling displaced seems to carry on down through generations. It may help you as a woman to prepare for the time when your son will bring home a woman as a wife to "displace" you.

I want to quickly address this displacement syndrome that many women suffer when their sons, brothers, and friends gets married and build their own homes. It will do us good as women to borrow a leaf from men, who hardly have problems with their new families after marriage. They seem to better accept the changes as a matter of course and settle into their new roles. We should not see those who marry our sons, brothers, or friends as competitors, intruders, and snatchers, when in fact we are gaining an addition to our family, as this new woman has capacities that will lead to a better family for your son or brother and the entire family. If she does well, she could become a source of pride and incredible support to your family. This way, everybody wins. As for the woman at the receiving end of such accusations, please always extend a hand of fellowship to members of your new family. Remember, you will be in their shoes some day!

Stop the Comparison

Learn not to compare yourself to the best others can do but to the best you can do. It will be more productive to help our husbands become the best God wants them to be instead of a copy of some other very good person.

It is God's prerogative to decide who He wants your husband to be so you can help him become that person. No one loves to be told he is a failure, especially when you always compare his achievements with those of others. You may even make the situation worse by telling him what Mr. Lagbaja has achieved, what Mr. Temedo has just become, or what Mr. Lakasigbo has bought for his wife. Women should desist from this keeping-up-with-the-Joneses behavior. Families should plan together what they want to achieve, instead of copying and comparing themselves with others, as this will fuel discord in the home, jealousy among friends, and unhealthy rivalry.

The comparison game could be blatant, as described above, or subtle, showing up in the way you make your requests, pass information to your husband or even the children, and a lot of our body language. We should encourage our husbands to do well, or improve if they are already doing well, but we should not damage their sense of self-worth and confidence by making scathing remarks and comments. They must not feel compelled to do wrong in order to meet our demands. I must

> You may even make the situation worse by telling him what Mr. Lagbaja has achieved, what Mr. Temedo has just become, or what Mr. Lakasigbo has bought for his wife.

quickly add that I expect every man to take care of his wife, even when the woman works outside the home; but this must be done according to their means, not according to our demands. Every woman who is or has the tendency to be demanding must overcome it.

THOUGHT AND PRAYER

I have the opportunity of a lifetime to cooperate with God in His quest to bless my husband. I will not compare my husband with any other man as I work with God in this venture.

Dear God, thank You for this privilege to work with You to achieve Your purpose. Help me to do it as best I can in all ways possible and at all times. In Jesus' name, amen.

Live, Love, Laugh, and Learn

It is so important to *live* in order to do any other thing! If you are reading this book, you are probably alive and can go on to live. My advice to live goes beyond being alive; it means enjoying being alive and living a purposeful life. If life has become a bore or a drag, it is time to rethink and redirect your thoughts and energy toward improving your life. Perhaps you want to turn your life into an amazing adventure or calm the storm raging in your heart. You have to live in order to love yourself, your husband, and even God! Living is an act of the will, and that decision can only be taken by you, with God's help.

If *love* is "working for the greatest good of another

person," then it has to be a deliberate act of the will, not a passive and perfunctory activity. Various writers have identified what may be called "the language of love," and it includes spending quality time together, giving affirmation through words, doing thoughtful acts of service, and extending physical touch. You and your spouse may find your own unique art and language that is cherished by both of you.

As for *laughter*, it does good—like medicine! Find things to laugh over, and learn to laugh at yourself but not at others, though poking slight fun at your friends may be allowed. A merry heart is a gift of God, and you can receive it as you cultivate a heart of gratitude and appreciate the beautiful people and lovely things around you. If you don't know where to start, thank God for all the beauty and creativity He has given to us through nature. Let those things remind you of His majesty, awesome power, everlasting care, and love. The more we appreciate, the more we are able to relax and enjoy what is around us. As we enjoy what is around us, we are able to have fun and laughter.

Learning is a lifelong quest for everyone, as there is no end to it. We can cultivate minds that are teachable. Learning is a process of action and replacement, and the poem below caught my attention concerning this:

> Because the world is hungry,
> go with bread.
> Because the world is filled with strife,
> go with peace.

Because the world is filled with deceptions
and lies,
go with truth.
Because the world would die without,
go with the love of God.

—Anonymous

Create a conducive environment for learning in your family by taking advantage of opportunities to learn new and better ways of doing things.

Are You in an Abusive Relationship? Apply Tough Love!

I will attempt to define what I mean by "tough love." It is the ability to take a decision that may seem to work against someone you love in the short run, in order to save them from further destruction in the long run. In applying tough love, the person you save from further destruction may not be your just husband; it may be you, the children, and other people who love both of you.

Exercise tough love, and let him know in a kind way that there will be consequences (such as you distancing yourself from him) if he continues to treat you in an angry, abusive way, either physically or emotionally. You must not cooperate with a man who abuses you by keeping quiet. Abuse thrives where it is kept hidden. An abusive partner must be exposed in order to help him know his behavior is unacceptable.

Perhaps you need to "feel needed" in order to feel loved and are willing to go to any lengths to keep a needy person dependent on you. Please seek counseling if this is the case. Some women in abusive relationships may be loyal to the point of being destructive both to themselves and others. You may need to allow an irresponsible person to face the consequences of his actions so he can come to his senses. You need to accept responsibility for yourself and work on your own growth and recovery from an abusive relationship. This book will not cover such details, so proper counseling is advised.

Applying tough love does not involve physically harming your man, but you must find someone he respects to speak to about his behavior, and you must make it clear that you will not accept abuse. Boundaries of good and acceptable behavior must be set very early in relationships. Setting boundaries does not mean ordering your spouse around or brandishing a list of dos and don'ts he must abide before he can have your hand in marriage. Rudeness, pride, and bad behavior are not part of a Christian's character, and we must not cultivate crudeness because we want to deal with a challenge.

THOUGHT AND PRAYER

My body is God's sanctuary, not a battlefield. It will not be debased or used as an outlet for wickedness by anyone. Jesus has sacrificed His life for humankind, so my life will not be sacrificed for anyone. I will not hide abuse or cooperate with anyone involved in it.

Eternal God, thank You as I become the woman You made me to be and help my husband become who You want him to become. Help me to always carry myself with the dignity worthy of the King's daughter. In Jesus' name, amen.

"Our most valuable possessions are those which can be shared without lessening, those which when shared multiply. Our least valuable possessions are those which when divided [shared] are diminished."
—William Danforth

Valuable Possessions

If you took a poll on what women consider their valuable possessions, the responses may surprise you. Answers could range from bank accounts to strings of degrees, their careers to their looks, and so on. William Danforth says about possessions: "Our most valuable possessions are those which can be shared without lessening, those which when shared multiply. Our least valuable possessions are those which when divided [shared] are diminished."[3] From this, we can learn that relationships that show love and commitment become some of our most valuable assets. Of course, it takes time to develop oneself; but having done so, of what benefit are one's endowments if used in one's own interest only? There is a generosity of soul that we, as women, need to cultivate to bring out the best in our relationships. As we develop a robust sense of self-worth, the fear of being taken for granted or treated badly by our spouses will fade and can be managed effectively.

THOUGHT AND PRAYER

I have been endowed with many valuable gifts, and now I am ready to use them in favor of my husband, children, and the society. I will not keep these endowments to myself and lose the joy of seeing others benefit from them.

Oh Lord, thank You for the gifts You endowed me with. Help me use them in favor of my family and others around me. In Jesus' name, amen.

Part Six

Sixteen

Work On Your Marriage "As Is"!

HAVE YOU EVER gone to inspect something for purchase at an auction and heard the term *as is*? It means that the item you would be buying is what you see right there before you, so you may decide whether to buy or not.

Thankfully, you did not buy your spouse; you married him—hopefully of your own volition. Now that you have entered into this union, please commit to making it good by working on it. The power of choice is one of the greatest gifts God gave to humans, and we can decide to use it positively to make our marriages and lives better. Thinking of making our lives better when our marriages are in trouble is an uphill task for anyone, most especially the woman.

> The most direct path to healing any relationship runs through the heart and soul of the person who has the most motivation to change.
> —Arlene Harder

To get the best out of a woman, her relationships at home must be in good condition. If we know this, then as women we must be wise enough to work for the interest of our marriages. The façade of having it all together in the office and crying yourself to sleep at night is not a smart option. Every woman reading this book should wise up.

If you do all you know to do and it is still not working, seek counseling, but do not give up on your marriage if it depends on you and if your life is not in danger. Have faith in the goodness and sovereignty of God while you do all you can. There is a silence that estrangement brings; it is like weeds taking over an untended garden. Some people freeze as life throws problems at them; they no longer respond or move forward. Please keep an open channel of communication with your spouse, even while a problem exists and is being addressed. If you are a woman in a flagging relationship, please dust off your sensuality and polish your once-radiant beauty, and get ready for another phase in your relationship with your husband.

> The most direct path to healing any relationship runs through the heart and soul of the person who has the most motivation to change.
>
> —ARLENE HARDER[1]

When that motivation is combined with courage, you are well on your way to healing, improving, and strengthening your relationship with your husband. As you probably know, it takes courage to sort through the many aspects of a difficult relationship and discover what you can do to make it better. It also takes courage to shift your focus from insisting that the other person must first change before your heart can heal. Not only that, it takes courage to recognize that the only person you can change is yourself. Above all, it takes courage to make any relationship work.

The undeniable fact is that you have to change yourself before you can lend a helping hand to another person who may need to change. When this opportunity presents itself, you cannot seize it; only your spouse can! Create the environment for change, and prayerfully watch him seize it. As he watches you change, he too begins to change without your direct intervention.

If you have noticed how I punctuate every sentence with the word "prayerful," it is because I know it is difficult to attain stability in a world as complex as this without an anchor in God. Prayerfully, laughter, hope, joy, and even romance will return to your marriage.

Women must commit to restoring unity and strength to the family by cultivating functional families. We must create a culture of using family ties to restore this unity and strength as a people of God and as a nation.

THOUGHT AND PRAYER

I have the capacity to make my relationship with my husband strong and mutually rewarding. I will not freeze and allow life to throw things at me. I will work in my best interest to make my family a happy and fulfilled unit.

Dear God, thank You for helping me come to the realization that I can be the best and get the best for my family. Please help me keep this in mind as I go about my daily activities. In Jesus' name, amen.

Your Past and Your Self-Worth

We all (or at least, most of us!) have past mistakes and tarnished attempts, but the good news is we can move ahead of these mistakes after learning from them. In fact, we can move on to something bigger, better, and glorious as God uses our regrets and lost opportunities to make us incredibly beautiful for Him.

As Elfrieda Nikkel said in an article, "Overwhelmed by Negative Feelings? There Is Something You Can Do About It," negative feelings may be there because of a conflict in your marriage, difficult work situations, problems with your children, financial difficulties, or just a feeling of hopelessness because life seems so unfair. Is there anything that can be done about these negative feelings? Can we control our feelings? Can we change them?[2]

If you were asked to make yourself feel happy, you would probably think of a wonderful experience you have had, like winning a prize or experiencing a special celebration. On the other hand, if you were asked to make yourself feel sad, you would think of a very devastating or sad experience. This tells us that our feelings are usually connected to our thoughts. Often, we cannot control the circumstances that lead to our thoughts, but we can choose how we want to think about them, and that in turn affects our feelings.

While we're at it, if anyone scoffs at you, please remember that, as T. D. Jakes says, "Criticism is a natural part of achieving greatness."[3]

When Something Goes Wrong

There are many things that can go wrong in any relationship, and marriage is no exception. Unexpectedly or expectedly, things go wrong in relationships sometimes, so a woman has to be sensitive to tell the spiritual and emotional temperature of her family. There are many things that could go wrong in a home, including everyday issues such as returning from work rather late and serious issues such as someone being involved in unwholesome behavior. Please do not fuel a deteriorating relationship by demonstrating your verbal prowess or self-righteousness. Try to understand the issue and nip it in the bud; that is why you are a woman endowed by God with wisdom and intuition.

Talking with some couples in preparation for this book, we discussed some things that went wrong in their marriages and how they coped with resolving the issues. The issues ranged

Please do not fuel a deteriorating relationship by demonstrating your verbal prowess or self-righteousness. Try to understand the issue and nip it in the bud; that is why you are a woman endowed by God with wisdom and intuition.

from childlessness and delayed conception to financial problems (especially when both spouses had no jobs), infidelity, differences in family background, inability to resolve differences quickly, and so on. Some couples had interferences from their family and friends, and some religious leaders suggested the dissolution of their marriage. I came to the conclusion that the problems couples face can be grouped into two categories: those external to the couple and those occurring between the couple,

External problems are usually resolved satisfactorily and without loss of affection and trust. On the other hand, problems that succeed in driving a wedge between the couple are more potent and dangerous. A prophet was prophesying doom to one of the couples I spoke with; it took divine help to prevent the marriage from breaking. If the couple concerned had allowed the issue to cause a division between them, the marriage would probably have hit the rocks. Whenever trust is threatened, a couple should sit together to nip it in the bud. This can be effectively done by couples, even with highly sensitive issues such as infidelity. Again, the place of maturity, love, and forgiveness is central to the successes recorded by these marriages. It is better to work on an issue than to allow your marriage deteriorate or break down. There is no problem that cannot be resolved if both partners are willing to cooperate and keep their marriages intact.

Serious Stuff

Sometimes the things that go wrong in marriages are serious or even life-threatening. Even in such times, there is grace for the godly woman. Some of these things have direct effects on our mental health as women, and it may be helpful to see how people who went through them coped. This is not to frighten anyone but to encourage us all to seek God's help, come what may.

When a Christian marriage unravels, many questions rise to the surface. Elizabeth Corcoran, in her article "The Unraveling of a Christian Marriage: Why I Stayed," gave many reasons why she did not walk out of her unraveling marriage. She says, "When I was a little girl, my parents divorced. I could probably stop writing right here. I was bound and determined to not repeat the cycle of divorce in my family." She had a sense of history and did not want to repeat or establish a cycle of divorce in her family line. She says:

> I thought God would answer my prayers. I prayed a lot. I prayed for God to change my spouse. I prayed for God to change me. I prayed for God to rearrange my expectations. I prayed for God to make me more selfless. And I hoped that God would answer my prayers and heal us.[4]

She had faith in God to heal her marriage.

> I was in a church. Community holds you together and holds you in place and keeps you from doing all sorts of things you might otherwise do if left to your own devices. My spouse and I began attending our current church two weeks after we got

> married, and we never looked anywhere
> else. We grew up there, basically. We
> had our children there. We served there.
> I worked there. We were known there.
> And when you let roots grow deep and
> people see inside your life and heart and
> you know you're going to see those same
> people another one or two times that week,
> it's really difficult to slide into a sin or
> completely walk away from what you know
> to be true without a bunch of people taking
> you to task. I knew that if I up and walked
> away, I'd have many people in my face—
> because they loved me—and if I stayed
> away, I'd probably lose my support system.
> I stayed because my church body takes care
> of its own and we try to protect each other
> from hurting ourselves.[5]

The church as a community of God's people should
form a support system that is a bulwark against family
decay and breakdown. We should protect and bear up
those hurting in our midst. I hope the church remains
alive to this responsibility, even in modern times and as
we live more private lifestyles.

She further said:

> I have two children. I believe to my core
> that it's my job to show my kids how to
> live as adults. I have failed miserably in
> this respect. But I wanted them to see

that what I said I believed—that marriage
is for a lifetime—matched what I actually
lived out, by actually staying married for a
lifetime. Children of divorce have a higher
marriage failure potential. I didn't want
to do that to my children, set them up for
failure before they even married. I stayed
because I didn't want my children to be
raised in a broken home.[6]

She gave so many other reasons why she fought to
keep her marriage, and God honored her faith. I believe
every woman should demonstrate this type of faith and
God will honor her, too.

In a story on sexual abuse, writer Karen Stiller talked
of "severe gifts." She said a severe gift is a very difficult
situation that God, in all His love, can actually use to
create something good in your life. Thank God that He
can use all situations in our lives.[7]

Barbara Epp, in her article "Up from Depression,"
describes what depression—in addition to feeling low and
discouraged—may be to those who suffer from it. She said
it may include the following:

- You feel desperate and that you are losing
  control of your life.
- You are in a space filled with darkness, fear,
  despair, and panic.
- Your thought world profoundly impacts your
  physical life.

- You feel as if time is either racing or you are moving in slow motion.
- Your world and activities appear insurmountable, and life feels like a pit.
- You have overwhelming feelings of isolation and feel disconnected from others.
- You feel trapped with no way to escape.
- You hate yourself for feeling the way you do and feel tremendous shame and guilt.[8]

She noted that depression is often triggered by trauma in our lives, which could be emotional, mental, social, physical, or a combination of any of these factors. She spoke of her experience as a young mother, struggling with a painful and severe post-partum depression that lasted seven years. The depression would be on and off, with the longest period lasting nine months. One thing she continued to do, though, was talk to God and cry out in her despair. As she stepped out in faith, believing the truths and principles that God had shown her, she began to realize God's plan for her life.

One woman battling cancer said:

> One of the things I most want to share is the difference God has made in my life. Each day with Him has been a fulfilling adventure. I haven't gained riches or fame as a result of my walk with God, but I have gained a richness of experience and a sense of significance and purpose that is worth far, far more.[9]

Use your network of friends if you cannot deal with your issues by yourself, especially if they are dire situations or things that threaten your mental health. Sometimes your friends cannot handle the issues because they do not have the experience needed. When this occurs, seek counsel.

Seeking Wise Counsel

Seeking counsel for a recurring problem is a good thing, but it is critical to be wise about where and who you seek counsel from. Sometimes we need to see an issue differently before we can get to the solution. We need a different perspective if a problem keeps recurring. You may need to look for someone who embodies the dignity, wisdom, and beauty befitting of your royal priesthood to relate to as a role model while seeking counsel. She does not have to know details when things are working well between you and your husband. And even when the rough patches show up, you have to decide when you have revealed enough to enable her give helpful and insightful counsel without making decisions for you. Proverbs 13:20 enjoins us to walk with the wise and become wise.

THOUGHT AND PRAYER

Every day, there are adequate emotional and other resources available to me to face the challenges of life and come out better than before. It is up to me to use these resources.

Heavenly Father, I will not be afraid of challenges but will face them using the various resources You have graciously provided. And I will triumph over these difficulties. In Jesus' name, amen.

When to Give Space

Divorce is not an option for the Christian couple, and with counsel a lot can be achieved to restore a broken relationship to one of love and trust. In this regard, when can a woman allow space between herself and her husband? By "space," I mean when a couple no longer sits to discuss and make decisions and no longer shares a bed. The most extreme case is when a wife has to escape from her husband because her life is in danger.

In situations where a relationship is strained, I suggest the woman takes the initiative to work for peace, as much as it lies within her power. Where this fails, please seek help from respected counselors and trusted friends. I believe if our tongues are tamed and our hearts tender toward our husbands, we can reach them, even in times of crises, because they know we love them.

In extreme situations, such as life and death, you surely need the intervention of family in addition to giving the man space. There are enough reasons to suggest that it is wise to seek help when peace breaks down totally. Too many women have lost their lives in their bid to stay in violent relationships. The newspapers are full of heart-rending stories of men who kill their wives after they have become estranged.

The statistics on domestic violence are daunting.

Domestic violence in Nigeria is on the up and up, with up to 50 percent of women claiming to have been battered by their husbands. Shockingly, more educated women (65 percent) are in this terrible situation as compared with their low income counterparts (55 percent). Most endure, believing they have nowhere to go and in any case, believing, for good reason, that the law will not protect them (a staggering 97.2 percent of them are not prepared to report to the police). Even in the few states that have passed laws against this insidious crime, the law is yet to be fully tested. Only recently, a twenty-nine-year-old banker was killed by her husband in a most gruesome manner. Before that, the scandalous story of wife battering by top diplomatic representatives and royal fathers have made the rounds, thus bringing the issue of spousal abuse once again to the front burner.

Hear what a victim of domestic violence sad:

> People still ask me till today, "Didn't you see the signs?" "For four years, surely you must have known he was violent and simply thought you could cope!" The answer is No! Nothing ever prepares one for domestic violence when it starts. The initial reaction is always shock and disbelief No matter who I tried to speak to about it, everybody told me to hush. "Do you want a failed marriage?" "Some men are just difficult," I was told. "Try not to annoy him" was another advice. I heeded all the advice and was determined to

love more, submit more, and do whatever it took to make the marriage work. No matter what I did, though, the raging incidents continued. It could be triggered by anything—a baby crying that I couldn't make keep quiet, a baby pooping in their diapers at an inconvenient time, resulting in an unpleasant smell, a handyman not finishing a job he had been asked to do on time....

This is when the physical violence graduated to an even higher level. Prior to this time, he had only been pelting me with objects, pushing, pulling, and dragging me by my clothes. Now the real beating started; we'd been married four years....

He pleaded again, saying he didn't want a divorce but would work at the marriage. He even cried....[10]

"Domestic violence should not happen to anybody. Ever. Period." This is the opening phrase on the domesticviolence. org website. It goes on to define it: "Domestic violence is about one person in a relationship using a pattern of behaviors to control the other person."

It could involve one or more of the following:

- Pushing, hitting, slapping, choking, kicking, or biting
- Threatening you, your children, other family members

- Threatening suicide to get you to do something
- Using or threatening to use a weapon against you
- Keeping or taking your paycheck
- Putting you down or making you feel bad
- Forcing you to have sex or to do sexual acts you do not want or like
- Keeping you from seeing your friends, family, or from going to work[11]

It is hard to know exactly how common domestic violence is. It may be an insidious phenomenon happening all around us without much attention being drawn to it and statistics are hard to come by, especially in Africa. There is unconfirmed news that it happens among both educated and uneducated women and among all age groups. There seems to be a code of silence being maintained by sufferers including lying to cover up telltale signs of physical abuse. It is not in the interest of any woman to cover up for an abusive partner. Rather it is important that every woman prevents herself from being abused.

United Nation's Fund for children (UNICEF) has taken special interest in the issue of domestic violence because of its negative effect on children and women. An editorial in its Innocenti Digest looks specifically at domestic violence building on the research carried out by the UNICEF Innocenti Research Centre for an earlier Digest on *Children and Violence*. It says:

> In recent years, there has been a greater understanding of the problem of domestic

violence, its causes and consequences, and an international consensus has developed on the need to deal with the issue. The Convention on the Elimination of All Forms of Discrimination against Women adopted by the United Nations General Assembly some 20 years ago, the decade-old Convention on the Rights of the Child, and the Platform for Action adopted at the Fourth International Conference on Women in Beijing in 1995, all reflect this consensus. But progress has been slow because attitudes are deeply entrenched and, to some extent, because effective strategies to address domestic violence are still being defined. As a result, women worldwide continue to suffer, with estimates varying from 20 to 50 per cent from country to country. This appalling toll will not be eased until families, governments, institutions and civil"....the digest demonstrates, domestic violence is a health, legal, economic, educational, developmental and, above all, a human rights issue.[12]

With such overwhelming voice against domestic violence, every abused person must take action by seeking immediate help. She must tell someone of her predicament from her family or the law before it gets out of hand. As more women break this oath of silence on domestic violence, it will drastically reduce. The Church has done a lot to tackle domestic violence yet more still needs to be done if the Christian marriage is to be an example to all who enter the institution of marriage.

Never allow your husband to beat you; and definitely never cooperate with him by keeping quiet if he ever beats you, even if only once. Men do not beat their wives because of what they do wrong; there is a deeper, underlying reason men beat women. If your husband beats you, it a sign that he lacks respect for womanhood, and especially for you his wife. Two consenting adults must be able to relate without physical or verbal abuse. Every woman must honor and respect her husband and earn her husband's respect too. Where respect is not being reciprocated, the underlying issue should be addressed as a matter of urgency to save the marriage.

THOUGHT AND PRAYER

I will cooperate with my husband to make our home happy and peaceful. However, I will not be treated disrespectfully by him nor agree to be beaten by him.

Dear God, thank You for giving me this man as my husband to make my life and his better. Thank You for not giving anyone the right to treat me badly or to take my life. Grant me the spirit of discernment to know when a drastic and life-threatening situation is developing and to take precautionary actions. I hide my life in You for Your own use and glory. In Jesus' name, amen.

Seventeen

Epilogue: A Tribute to Dennis

ENNIS AMIOKHAI IS my husband of thirty-three years. We have come a long way and have grown to love and respect each other deeply. Before I met him, I used to think I was a quiet person, but he shattered that myth. He is the person I respect most in the whole world, and he maintains an influence in our home even with very few words.

Some time ago, one of our sons told me, I think in exasperation, "Mummy, when you drive a car to the gate of our house, you hoot so many times before someone opens the gate. When daddy gets to the gate, he hoots just once and waits for the gate to be opened." I was surprised; I hope you believe me when I say that I don't count the number of times

I don't always wait to respond to issues; I "create" necessary action! Sometimes I want things to go faster, whereas he is saying to take it easy and go slower, slower. And then we reach a balance. Sometimes he stands on the sideline as I zoom past, full of energy and

daring activity! At other times, he stands like a rock in my way, preventing any further action. We have mastered the cues in managing whichever of these scenarios plays out.

I hoot for the gate to be opened. I made a mental note that I would try to reduce the number of times I hoot to maybe two or three—but to hoot once? No way! But these people love me to bits in spite of my numerous hoots!

My husband often tells me that whenever he enters a place where I am, he can feel me and know when everything is fine. He is a highly disciplined person with a Spartan lifestyle, and—wait for this—he is a loner. I learned this very early in marriage when I used to expect him to tag along as we attended all the first birthday parties of our friends' children! He would have none of this. After a while, I finally got the message and, reluctantly, let him be.

Since you now know who does more talking, I hope you do not think I did all the talking and the chasing before we got married. He did the full compliments of chasing and writing, and some of those letters were competing favorably with the Song of Solomon! I don't know how he mustered all the energy to give me such a hard chase before I agreed to marry him. He came into our marriage even more determined than I was to make a success of it, but I have since overtaken him.

Although I had no idea what the

future would be, I was attracted enough to want to share it with him. This attraction has been an enduring part of our relationship. We have faced many trying times together, but we do not allow any problems to come between us. No matter how emotive the issues, we have always chosen to face them together instead of allowing them to drive us apart. I should say that when we got married, we were not friends; we were more of lovers. Sensing the need to close this gap with his starry-eyed wife, he "applied," through a poem, asking to be my friend. We have been working at it since then, sometimes with exhilarating success—and at other times we are simply bewildered!

On the way to this very good place we find ourselves now, we have had to learn to understand each other and maximize the benefits of our differences. Not being one to pass up on good opportunities, I don't always wait to respond to issues; I "create" necessary action! Sometimes I want things to go faster, whereas he is saying to take it easy and go slower, slower. And then we reach a balance. Sometimes he stands on the sideline as I zoom past, full of energy and daring activity! At other times, he stands like a rock in my way, preventing any further action. We have mastered the cues in managing whichever of these scenarios plays out.

He has come a long way in his Christian commitment and relationships. However, we have not reached our destination yet; I still look forward to his being able to relate more warmly with people and to fellowship better. When we celebrated our tenth wedding anniversary and were reviewing our marriage, I asked what his best achievement in the marriage was. He told me his best decision in those ten years was in not attempting to change me. He allowed me be myself and grow into God's plan and purpose for me unhindered. Of course, I have changed only for the better, bringing so much verve into whatever I do. He remains the single most influential person that affects my capacity to give like a "flower opening to the sun." This freedom has made it possible to do the things God has laid on my heart to do. As an advocate for a good cause, this is exemplary.

I will let you in on a secret. In our room, we have a picture we have carried along with us wherever we have moved. It has two birds and the caption, "Love is two hearts with one song." This summarizes our lives together. I have implicit trust that he always works in my favor and in favor of our children, and I dare to think he believes the same about me. I still pledge, with God's help, unalloyed love, commitment, and loyalty to him.

If you like what this woman has become, now you know who to praise God for!

A Final Charge: Invitation to the Wedding Feast of the Lamb

We have spent some time together examining how to love our husbands forever. But there is a marriage that is even more enduring than the one we share with our husbands, and it is in your best interest to value this relationship above all others. It is the marriage of the Lamb to His bride, the church of God. In Ephesians 5:25–30 Paul likened marriage between a man and woman to the relationship between Jesus Christ and the church. In Revelation 19:6–9, we read about this wedding event, which is preceded by the coming of our Lord Jesus Christ:

> Then I heard again what sounded like the shouting of a huge crowd, or like the waves of a hundred oceans crashing on the shore, or like the mighty rolling of great thunder, "Praise the Lord. For the Lord our God, the Almighty reigns.
>
> Let us be glad and rejoice and honor him; for the wedding banquet of the Lamb, and his bride had prepared herself.
>
> She is permitted to wear the cleanest and whitest and finest of linen" fine linen represents the good deeds done by the people of God.
>
> And the Angel dictated this sentence to me: "Blessed are those who are invited to the wedding feast of the lamb." And he added, "God himself has stated this."

In Revelation 19:7, John recorded part of the loud proclamation of a huge crowd in heaven; and in verse 8, he continues, saying that the bride is permitted to wear the whitest and finest of linen. This represents the good deeds of God's people, and verse 9 says that those invited to the wedding feast are blessed.

A study of Revelation 5–7, 12–15, 17, 19, and 21–22 clearly indicates that the Lamb is Jesus Christ, the King of kings and Lord of lords who shed His blood to cleanse sinners. Romans 7:4, 2 Corinthians 11:2, and Ephesians

5:22–23 indicate that the bride of the Lamb is the Church. In light of these, it is evident that Revelation 19:7–9 is referring to the marriage of Jesus Christ to the church and the subsequent wedding feast. Every Christian must prepare for the Second Coming of the Lord and the marriage feast of the Lamb.

Are you a bride of Christ, the one without spot or wrinkle? Dr. James Merrit, a preacher, said: "The greatest temptation you will ever face is to die without Jesus Christ. Don't yield to it!"

Even so, Lord Jesus, come!

Maybe all of this sounds so strange and confusing to you. If you have never asked for forgiveness for your sins and salvation through the finished work of Jesus Christ on the cross, then you must do this right now. Please pray this prayer:

> *Lord Jesus, I confess my sins and the need for You to forgive me and make me an overcomer. I ask You to be the Lord and Master of my life. I want to be part of the events of the Last Days and the marriage of the Lamb. All these I ask in Jesus' name, amen.*

If you made this prayer commitment, please get in touch by sending an e-mail to howtoseries7@gmail.com.

Notes

Chapter One

1. Statistics retrieved from FCT High Court, Maitama, Abuja.

2. Gina Serpe, "Kim Kardashian and Kris Humphries Divorce: Anatomy of a Split," 2011, E!Online, http://www.eonline.com/news/272530/kim-kardashian-and-kris-humphries-divorce-anatomy-of-a-split (accessed August 6, 2012).

3. Amy Brewster, "Con: Divorce Rates Prove Marriage is No Fairy Tale," *The Pioneer Online*, California State University, http://thepioneeronline.com/editorials/2011/11/condivorce-rates-prove-marriage-is-no-fairy-tale/ (accessed August 13, 2012).

4. Fathers' Manifesto & Christian Party, "World Divorce Rates," 2010, http://www.fathersmanifesto.net/divorceworld.htm (accessed August 13, 2012).

5.   Carol T. Mowbray, *Women and Mental Health: New Directions for Change*. Routledge Mental Health, 1985, 11.

6.   Joe Burton, "Why Men Are Seldom Depressed," 2011, http://www.funnyordie.com/articles/2b7d61cfe8/why-men-are-seldom-depressed (accessed August 6, 2012).

7.   Kevin Miller, "Two Keys to a Happy Marriage," 2011, http://thoughts-about-god.com/family/km-happy-marriage.html (accessed August 6, 2012).

8.   Retrieved from http://tamsworld.blogspot.com/2005/08/characteristics-of-good-woman.html (accessed August 6, 2012).

Chapter Two

1.   Arlene Harder, "The Marriage Contract Game," 2002, http://www.support4change.com/index.php?option=com_content&view=article&id=95:marriage-contract-game&catid=54:finding-perfect-mate&Itemid=106 (accessed August 6, 2012).

Chapter Four

1.   Stormie Omartian, *The Power of a Praying Wife* (Eugene, OR: Harvest House Publishers, 1997), 13.

Chapter Five

1.   Stacy Wiebe, "The Power of a Mother's Promise," 2002, http://www.thoughts-about-god.com/stories/swpromises.htm (accessed August 6, 2012).

Chapter Six

1. Retrieved from www.literaturecollection.com/a/lord-byron/don-juan/10/ (accessed August 13, 2012).

Chapter Eight

1. Richard Innes, "Communicate, Communicate, Communicate," http://www.actsweb.org/articles/article.php?i=867&d=2&c=3 (accessed August 6, 2012).

Chapter Nine

1. Donald W. McCullough, *Mastering Personal Growth* (Colorado Springs, CO: Multnomah, 1992). Retrieved from http://seekingpeaceinastorm.blogspot.com/2011/06/you've-got-friend-in-me.html (accessed August 6, 2012).

2. Richard Innes, "The Art of Staying in Love," http://www.actsweb.org/articles/printer.php?i=35&d=1&p=2 (accessed August 6, 2012).

3. Ibid.

4. Retrieved from http://www.ourchurch.com/view/?pageID=160811 (accessed August 6, 2012).

Chapter Ten

1. Engineer Clement and Dr. Yetunde Oke, in discussion with the author.

2. John W. Gardner, *Excellence: Can We Be Equal and Excellent Too?* (New York: Harper & Brothers, 1961), 86.

Chapter Eleven

1.   Thomas Firminger Thiselton-Dyer, *Folk-lore of Women* (Chicago, IL: A.C. McClurg & Co., 1906), 5.

2.   Richard Innes, "Blame Game or Wise Choice," http://www.actsweb.org/articles/article.php?i=689&d=2&c=4 (accessed August 6, 2012).

3.   Elfrieda Nikkel, "Did You Know You're Someone Special?" Thoughts About God, http://www.thoughts-about-god.com/stories/en_special.html (accessed August 13, 2012).

4.   Ibid.

Chapter Twelve

1.   Retrieved from http://commonquote.com/author/4054/steve-farrar (accessed August 13, 2012).

2.   Retrieved from http://www.motivationalwellbeing.com/belief-quotes.html (accessed August 6, 2012).

3.   Jagan Krishnaraj, "Value of a Relationship in a Marriage," *Live Positive Way*, 2011, http://www.livepositiveway.com/2011_06_01_archive.html (accessed August 6, 2012).

Chapter Thirteen

1.   Nancy Leigh DeMoss, *Choosing Gratitude: Your Journey to Joy* (Chicago, IL: Moody Publishers, 2009), 68. Retrieved from http://reneeannsmith.com/a/top-5-new-years-resolutions-3/ (accessed August 13, 2012).

2.   Retrieved from http://www.quoteland.com/topic/Motivational-Quotes/232/ (accessed August 6, 2012).

3. Retrieved from www.wisdomword.info/dr-irwin-sarason/ (accessed August 6, 2012).

4. Elisabeth Corcoran, "The Unraveling of a Christian Marriage: Why I Stayed," 2011, http://www.crosswalk.com/family/marriage/divorce-and-remarriage/the-unraveling-of-a-christian-marriage-why-i-stayed.html (accessed August 6, 2012).

Chapter Fifteen

1. Richard Innes, "Lessons from Trees," http://www.actsweb.org/articles/article.php?i=250&d=2&c=5 (accessed August 13, 2012).

2. Herbert and Zelmyra Fisher, 2010, retrieved from http://twitter.com/longestmarried (accessed August 6, 2012).

3. Retrieved from www.allthingswilliam.com/sharing.html (accessed August 13, 2012).

Chapter Sixteen

1. Retrieved from http://www.support4change.com/index.php?option=com_content&view=article&id=139&Itemid=69 (accessed August 6, 2012).

2. Elfrieda Nikkel, "Overwhelmed by Negative Feelings? There is Something You Can Do About It," *Thoughts About God*, http://www.thoughts-about-god.com/stories/en_special.html (accessed August 13, 2012).

3. T.D. Jakes, *God's Leading Lady* (New York: G.P. Putnam's Sons, 2002).

4. Elisabeth Corcoran, "The Unraveling of a Christian Marriage: Why I Stayed," 2011, http://www

.crosswalk.com/family/marriage/divorce-and-remarriage/
the-unraveling-of-a-christian-marriage-why-i-stayed.html
(accessed August 6, 2012).

5. Ibid.

6. Ibid.

7. Karen Stiller, ed., "Jane Doe's Story," *Thoughts
About God*, www.thoughts-about-god.com/stories/jane_
doe.htm (accessed August 13, 2012).

8. Barbara Epp, "Up From Depression," *Thoughts
About God*, www.thoughts-about-god.com/stories/epp_b
.htm (accessed August 13, 2012).

9. Diane Willis, "Bloom...Where You Are Planted,"
Thoughts About God, www.thoughts-about-god.com/
stories/diane_w.htm (accessed August 13, 2012).

10. Tess Wigwe, "Domestic Violence: When the
Law Fails to Protect," *This Day Live*, September 20, 2011,
http://www.thisdaylive.com/articles/domestic-violence
-when-the-law-fails-to-protect/98863/ (accessed August
13, 2012).

11. Retrieved from www.domesticviolence.org
(accessed August 13, 2012).

12. Mehr Khan, "Domestic Violence Against
Women and Girls," *UNICEF Innocenti Digest*, no. 6
(2000): 1, http://www.unicef-irc.org/publications/pdf/
digest6e.pdf (accessed August 13, 2012).

About the Author

Olapeju Otsemobor is the team leader and chief executive officer of Wajomate Limited, a project management and training outfit. She is a worshiper and testifier to the power of God, as well as a deacon in the New Estate Baptist Church in Abuja, Nigeria. She and her husband, Dennis, have three children.

Contact the Author

E-mail: howtoseries7@gmail.com